# Dubai mini

## The Essential **VisItors'** Guide

**Dubai mini Explorer**
ISBN – 978-9948-8586-1-4

Front cover photograph: Sheikh Zayed Road – Victor Romero

Printed and bound by
Emirates Printing Press, Dubai, UAE

**Explorer Publishing & Distribution**
PO Box 34275, Dubai , United Arab Emirates
Phone (+971 4) 340 8805   Fax (+971 4) 340 8806
Email info@explorerpublishing.com
Web www.explorerpublishing.com

# Introduction

The *Dubai Mini Explorer* is a pocket-sized parcel of essential information that will help you make the most of your trip to this glorious city. It covers sights, culture, history, activities and the best places for eating and drinking. It is written by Dubai residents, and brought to you by the same team responsible for the *Dubai Explorer: The Complete Residents' Guide*. If you want to know more about what we do, or tell us what we've missed, go to www.explorerpublishing.com.

The Dubai Mini Explorer

**Editorial Team:** Helen Spearman, Jakob Marsico, Sean Kearns, Ingrid Cupido
**Designers:** Hashim Moideen, Jayde Fernandes, Rafi VP
**Photographers:** Victor Romero, the Explorer team, Ahmed Alshehi

# Contents

# Essentials

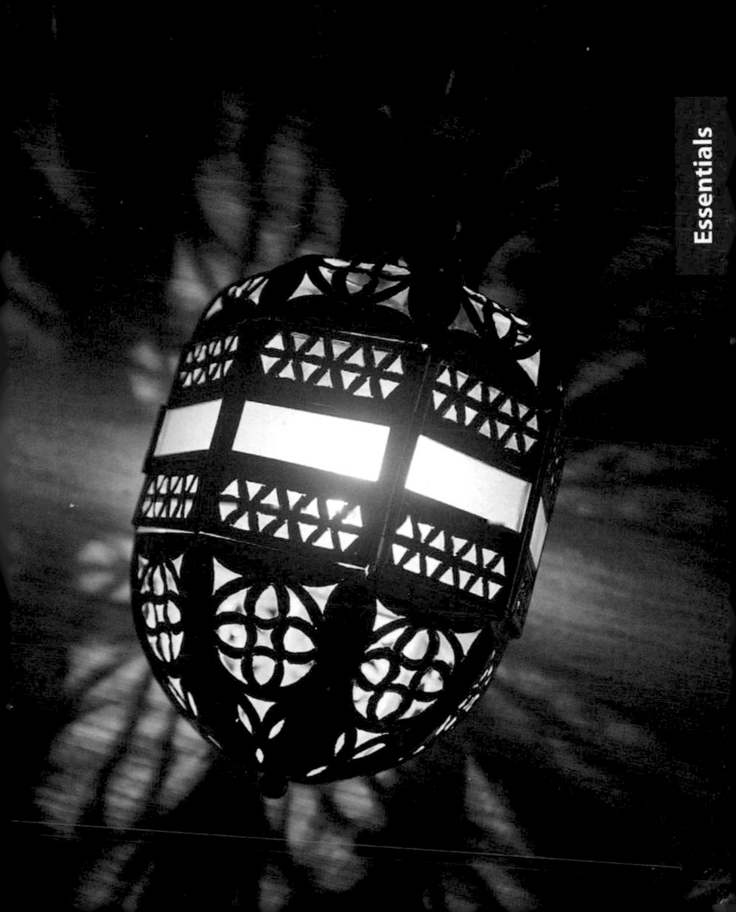

# Essentials

## Welcome to a city of stark contrasts; of sand dunes and skyscrapers, camels and fast cars, museums and malls. Welcome to Dubai.

Whatever your reason for touching down in this desert metropolis, it's hard not to captivated by its growth and unshakeable ambition. The world's tallest building is already here, and a slew of new towers and whole cities are not far behind. Yet underneath the shiny surface there is more to Dubai than cranes and five-star cliche: you'll find Emiratis, fresh-faced expats, corporate climbers, and sunburnt tourists all enjoying and exploring the many sides to a surprisingly multi-layered city.

As you'd expect from a truly international destination, there is a wide scope of activities, cuisines and adventures to be had, many at prices that you wouldn't expect from the 'seven-star' headlines. Try dining in Arabic street cafes (p.172), browsing the souks (p.152) and haggling for souvenirs (p.172) to get a sense of local tradition, or sample Dubai's plethora of malls (p.156), upmarket hotels (p.47) and fine-dining restaurants (p.174) for a taste of its luxury reputation.

Outside of the city is a whole new set of landscapes and a more traditional way of life. Seemingly endless vistas of untouched sand dunes are just waiting to be explored, so pile into that Land Cruiser and take a tour (p.108). Further out, the East Coast (p.106) of the UAE is a haven for divers and

Sheikh Zayed Road

snorkellers, and the delights of Oman's rugged Musandam peninsula are only an hour or so north.

Over the next few pages you'll find vital information to help you plan your trip, plus advice on what to do when you first arrive. The things that you really shouldn't miss start on the next page. The Exploring chapter (p.52) divides the city up, highlighting each area's best bits, such as museums, galleries and heritage sites. In Sports & Spas (p.118) you'll find out what the city has to offer for sports fans, keen golfers, and those who simply prefer to be pampered. Shopping (p.140) is your detailed guide to malls, boutiques and souks.

Going Out (p.172) will help you manoeuvre your way through Dubai's increasingly impressive maze of restaurants, bars and clubs, while Profile (p.246) puts it all in context.

# Dubai Checklist

## 01 Ski Dubai

This impressive indoor slope, jutting out of Mall of the Emirates (p.162), has two enjoyable runs, complete with real snow, and a snow park where you can try tobogganing. Lessons are available for beginners, and there's even a cafe halfway up the 'piste'. See p.97.

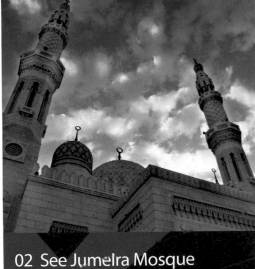

## 02 See Jumelra Mosque

This is one of Dubai's most picturesque mosques and one of the few open to non-Muslims. Learn more about local culture, Islam and what goes on inside this place of worship through organised tours held four days a week at 10:00 sharp. See p.80.

## 03 Tackle The Dunes

A trip to the desert is a must during your stay in Dubai. Surfing over the dunes in a car at impossible angles is great fun – as is a camel ride, eating your fill at a barbecue and learning how to belly dance. Tour operators are plentiful and professional. See p.108.

## 04  Sample The Souks

Still an essential part of life for many people, Dubai's souks are a welcome slice of tradition. Check out the Spice Souk (p.154), the colourful textile souk in Bur Dubai (p.154), the Fish Market in Deira (p.64) and the world-renowned Gold Souk (p.153).

## 05 Experience The Burj

The spark behind Dubai's current boom, the epitome of ostentation and an architectural masterpiece, the Burj Al Arab is the city's mascot. See for yourself what the fuss is about with either afternoon tea at Sahn Eddar (p.237) or a meal at Al Mahara (p.236).

## 06 Take A Bus Tour

View the city from the upper floor of a double decker bus, learning some fascinating facts about Dubai along the way. The Big Bus Company (p.110) allows you to hop on and off at various attractions, while the amphibious Wonder Bus takes to water (p.110).

## 07 Hit The Malls

Dubai does shopping bigger, better and cheaper than
most. So whether it's to beat the heat or browse the
growing number of boutiques, you won't be short
of options. See p.156 for a full guide to the city's
shopping hotspots.

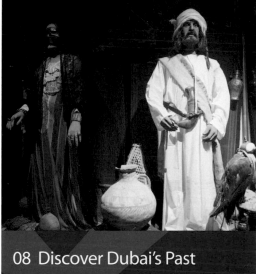

## 08 Discover Dubai's Past

Dubai Museum is an enjoyable space that offers an enlightening stroll through the city's history. Displays depict everything from the fascinating story of the emirate to the wildlife and natural environment of the UAE. See p.59.

## 09 Explore Madinat Jumeirah

Lose yourself exploring the maze of alleyways of this traditionally styled, air-conditioned souk, leading to intimate open-fronted boutiques, upmarket cafes, and charming waterfront bars and restaurants. A modern-day Arabian experience not to be missed. See p.165.

# 10 Smoke Shisha

Join in the Arabic social tradition and while away some hours at a shisha cafe. 'Nargile' (to give its official name) is a mixture of tobacco, molasses and a variety of fruity flavourings, which is smoked from a water pipe. See p.254 to perfect your technique.

Best Of Dubai

# For Adrenaline Junkies

You can see the growing metropolis from the sky while parasailing (p.127) at one of the many beachside hotels or treat yourself to a helicopter tour (p.112). Take it a step further – literally – and jump out of a plane at Umm Al Quwain Aeroclub (www.uaqaeroclub.com) where a tandem skydive from 12,000 feet costs Dhs.800.

Dune bashing is a great way to clear the cobwebs and see some spectacular desert vistas. If you go with a tour group, (p.128) sand skiing or boarding might be on offer too. If you want to get behind the wheel you'll find dune buggies and quad biking on the road to Hatta (p.105). If it's too hot then head to Dubai Autodrome (www.dubaiautodrome.com) for a karting race around the 1.2km track. Those who prefer water to sand can get a buzz from kayaking, snorkelling, surfing, diving or waterskiing. See p.129 for more details.

# For Big Spenders

Dubai's vast array of activities and shops will make even the largest of wallets wince. So where to start? Check in to the finest hotel you can afford (p.46), then head to dinner cooked by a celeb chef; choose from Marco Pierre White at Frankie's (p.198), Gary Rhodes at Rhodes Mezzanine (p.201) or Gordon Ramsay at Verre (p.195). A few drinks at Buddha Bar (p.202) or cocktails at Vu's Bar (p.233) should account for any spare change. Speed up recovery at one of Dubai's impressive spas (p.118) then hit the shops: Emirates Towers (p.156) has the best line-up of designer labels, Mall of the Emirates (p.162) and Deira City Centre (p.158) have everything else.

## For Culture Buffs

Delve beneath its glamorous exterior and you'll find the Dubai of old. Try Middle Eastern cuisine (p.174), explore the souks (p.152), travel on an abra (p.45), see the dhow wharfage (p.67) and learn the history at Dubai Museum (p.59). There are authentic souvenirs to be found (p.172), while the art and gallery scene is keeping pace with the skyscrapers. Visit B21 (p.96) and The Jam Jar (p.97), or to really immerse yourself in the art world stay at XVA Gallery (p.61).

## For Foodies

Dubai offers a curious mix of American fastfood staples, Lebanese street cafes and fine-dining hotel restaurants, but while in town it is the cheap, delicious Arabic food that should be top of your list. Try shawarmas, falafel, hummus, and tabbouleh, all washed down with the finest fresh juices. See p.182 for the pick of the bunch.

## For Water Babies

You may want an action-packed stay or perhaps the thought of turning this page is a little strenuous. Either way, there's plenty of choice. From relaxing at the hotel pool and Jumeirah Beach Park (p.79) to diving, snorkelling and sailing (p.129), fans of being on, in or by the water will be in aqua heaven. Dubai has a pretty active surf scene, while most of the beach-side hotels offer watersports including parasailing, jetskiing and being thrown around on inflatable rings. If you have rented a car and want to spot some marine life then a trip to the East Coast (p.106) is a must.

# Visiting Dubai

**The UAE warmly welcomes visitors, but has a few rules and regulations that require extra attention. Read on for the vital information.**

## Getting There

Dubai International Airport (DXB) is an important global hub, and handled more than 34 million passengers in 2007. A $540 million expansion programme will see a third terminal added in 2009, solely for use by Emirates, Dubai's rapidly expanding airline. Currently, more than 120 airlines use the airport, flying to over 200 destinations. Terminal 1 handles major international airlines. Queues for check-in and departure are bearable, although it can take a while to get through passport control. The airport is clean and modern, facilities are good, and there's a huge duty free section on the lower floor. For up-to-date flight information call 04 216 6666.

### Al Maktoum Airport

**Construction is well underway on Dubai's second airport (Al Maktoum International Airport). The first phase is expected to open in 2008, although it will cater only for freight. But by 2050 the airport will have the capacity to handle 120 million passengers a year.**

## Airport Transfer

If you booked your break through a hotel or travel agency, it's likely that pick-up from the airport will

Deira

be included. If not, there is an airport bus to and from Dubai International Airport every 30 minutes, 24 hours a day. There are two loop routes: Route 401 services Deira, while Route 402 serves Bur Dubai. The fare is Dhs.3. Call 800 9090 for details, or log on to www.rta.ae.

Taxis leaving from the airport charge an extra Dhs.25 so it will cost approximately Dhs.45 in total for a journey to the hotels of Sheikh Zayed Road or up to Dhs.80 to Dubai Marina. The stand is straight in front of you as you leave arrivals.

## Airlines

| | | |
|---|---|---|
| Aer Lingus | 04 316 6752 | www.aerlingus.com |
| Air Arabia | 06 508 8888 | www.airarabia.com |
| Air France | 02 294 5899 | www.airfrance.co.ae |
| American Airlines | 04 393 3234 | www.aa.com |
| British Airways | 04 307 5777 | www.britishairways.com |
| Emirates | 04 214 4444 | www.emirates.com |
| Etihad Airways | 02 505 8000 | www.etihadairways.com |
| Gulf Air | 04 271 3222 | www.gulfairco.com |
| KLM Royal Dutch Airlines | 04 319 3777 | www.klm.com |
| Lufthansa | 04 316 6642 | www.lufthansa.com |
| Oman Air | 04 351 8080 | www.oman-air.com |
| Qatar Airways | 04 229 2229 | www.qatarairways.com |
| Royal Brunei Airlines | 04 351 9330 | www.bruneiair.com |
| Royal Jet Group | 02 575 7000 | www.royaljetgroup.com |
| Singapore Airlines | 04 223 2300 | www.singaporeair.com |
| South African Airways | 04 397 0766 | www.flysaa.com |
| United Airlines | 04 316 6942 | www.ual.com |
| Virgin Atlantic | 04 406 0600 | www.virgin-atlantic.com |

# Visas & Customs

Requirements vary depending on your country of origin. Regulations should be checked before departure. GCC nationals (Bahrain, Kuwait, Qatar, Oman and Saudi Arabia) do not need a visa to enter Dubai. Citizens from many other countries get an automatic visa upon arrival at the airport (see box right for the full list). The entry visa is valid for 60 days, although you can renew for a further 30 days. For those travelling onwards to a destination other than that of the original departure, a special transit visa (up to 96 hours) may be obtained free of charge through certain airlines.

Certain prescription medications are banned even though they are freely available over the counter in other countries. High-profile cases have highlighted the UAE's zero tolerance to drugs. Even a miniscule quantity in your possession could result in a lengthy jail term. Bags will be scanned to ensure you have no offending magazines or DVDs.

## Visa On Arrival

Citizens of the following countries receive an automatic visa on arrival: Andorra, Australia, Austria, Belguim, Brunei, Canada, Cyprus, Denmark, Finland, France, Germany, Greece, Hong Kong, Iceland, Ireland, Italy, Japan, Liechtenstein, Luxembourg, Malaysia, Malta, Monaco, Netherlands, New Zealand, Norway, Portugal, San Marino, Singapore, South Korea, Spain, Sweden, Switzerland, United Kingdom, United States of America and Vatican City.

# Climate

Dubai has a subtropical and arid climate. Sunny blue skies and high temperatures can be expected most of the year. Rainfall is infrequent and erratic, usually falling on an average of only 25 days per year, mainly in winter (December to March). Temperatures range from a low of around 10°C (50°F) in winter to a high of 48°C (118°F) in summer. The mean daily maximum is 24°C (75°F) in January, rising to 41°C (106°F) in August. Humidity is usually between 50% and 65%, and is slightly lower in the summer than the winter. However, when combined with the high summer temperatures, even 60% humidity can produce extremely uncomfortable conditions. The most pleasant time to visit Dubai is in the cooler winter months when temperatures are perfect for comfortable days on the beach and long, lingering evenings outside. For up-to-date weather reports, see www.dubaiairport.com/dubaimet, or www.dubaitourism.co.ae.

# Crime & Safety

While the crime rate in Dubai is very low, a healthy degree of caution should still be exercised. Keep your valuables and travel documents locked in your hotel room or in the safe. When in crowds, be discreet with your money and wallet and don't carry large amounts of cash on you.

With a multitude of driving styles converging on Dubai's roads, navigating the streets either on foot or in a vehicle can be a challenge. When walking, you need to be conscious of the traffic as drivers often don't give pedestrians the space or consideration you might be used to. When crossing roads use designated pedestrian crossings wherever possible (jaywalking is actually illegal), and make sure all cars are going to stop before you cross.

## Dos & Don'ts

The UAE is one of the most tolerant and liberal states in the region, but as a guest in a Muslim country you should act accordingly. Lewd and drunken behaviour is not only disrespectful but can lead to arrest and detention. Women should be aware that revealing clothing can attract unwanted attention, so very short skirts and strapless tops should be avoided. Malls have recently put up signs making it clear that inappropriate clothing and public displays of affection are not allowed. With prices for cigarettes low, smoking is very common. However, new laws have banned lighting up in malls and some restaurants so it's best to check the policy before striking up.

There's zero tolerance towards drink driving, even after one pint. With thousands of low-fare taxis available there is no excuse or need. A month-one prison sentence awaits those who offend.

## Electricity & Water

The electricity supply is 220/240 volts and 50 cycles. Most hotel rooms and villas use the three-pin plug that is the universal in the UK. Adaptors are widely available and only cost a few dirhams. Tap water is desalinated sea water and is perfectly safe to drink although most people choose mineral water because it tastes better. Bottled water is cheap, especially local brands such as Masafi. Bottled water, both local and imported, is served in hotels and restaurants.

# Female Visitors

The UAE is incredibly progressive in comparison to some of its neighbours. Women are generally safe, but may feel uncomfortable with the amount of staring they will experience, especially on beaches and in the souks. The attention is merely curiosity and rarely turns into anything dangerous, but can be unpleasant nonetheless. It is best just to ignore it. However, avoid excessively tight or revealing clothing as a matter of respect as much as anything else. Police officers are very helpful and happy to deal with complaints. Taxis exclusively for women are available (p.44).

# Language

Arabic is the official language of the UAE, although English, Hindi, Malayalam and Urdu are commonly spoken. Most road signs, shop signs and restaurant menus are in English and Arabic. The further out of town you go, the more you will find just Arabic, both spoken and on street and shop signs. Arabic isn't the easiest language to pick up, or to pronounce. But if you can throw in a couple of words here and there, you're likely to receive a smile – even if your pronunciation is terrible.

# Lost & Found

To avoid a great deal of hassle if your personal documents go missing, make sure you keep one photocopy with friends or family back home and one copy in a secure place, such as a safe. If you have no luck, then try Dubai Police (999) or the Department for Tourist Security (800 4438 – toll free) to report the loss or theft. They will advise you on a course of action. If you've lost something in a taxi, call the relevant taxi company (p.44). If you lose your passport, your next stop should be your embassy or consulate. See the website table (p.34) for embassy listings.

## Basic Arabic

### General

| | |
|---|---|
| Yes | na'am |
| No | la |
| Please | min fadlak (m)/min fadliki (f) |
| Thank you | shukran |
| Praise be to God | al-hamdu l-illah |
| God willing | in shaa'a l-laah |

### Greetings

| | |
|---|---|
| Greeting (peace be upon you) | as-salaamu alaykom |
| Greeting (in reply) | wa alaykom is salaam |
| Good morning | sabah il-khayr |
| Good morning (in reply) | sabah in-nuwr |
| Good evening | masa il-khayr |
| Good evening (in reply) | masa in-nuwr |
| Hello | marhaba |
| Hello (in reply) | marhabtayn |
| How are you? | kayf haalak (m)/kayf haalik (f) |
| Fine, thank you | zayn, shukran (m)/zayna, shukran (f) |

| Welcome | ahlan wa sahlan |
| Goodbye | ma is-salaama |
| Introduction | |
| My name is... | ismiy... |
| What is your name? | shuw ismak (m) / shuw ismik (f) |
| Where are you from? | min wayn inta (m) / min wayn |
| Questions | |
| How many / much? | kam? |
| Where? | wayn? |
| When? | mataa? |
| Which? | ayy? |
| How? | kayf? |
| What? | shuw? |
| Why? | laysh? |
| And | wa |
| Numbers | |
| Zero | sifr |
| One | waahad |
| Two | ithnayn |
| Three | thalatha |
| Four | arba'a |
| Five | khamsa |
| Six | sitta |
| Seven | saba'a |
| Eight | thamaanya |
| Nine | tiss'a |
| Ten | ashara |

# Money

Cash is still the preferred method of payment, although credit and debit cards are now widely accepted. Foreign currencies and travellers' cheques can be exchanged in licensed exchange offices, banks and hotels (as usual, a passport is required for exchanging travellers' cheques). If you're shopping in the souks and markets in Dubai, or in smaller shops, you're better off paying cash even if a shop does accept other forms of payment as it will help your bargaining power.

The monetary unit is the dirham (Dhs.), which is divided into 100 fils. The currency is also referred to as AED (Arab Emirate dirham). Notes come in denominations of Dhs.5 (brown), Dhs.10 (green), Dhs.20 (light blue), Dhs.50 (purple), Dhs.100 (pink), Dhs.500 (blue) and Dhs.1,000 (browny-purple). The denominations are indicated on the notes in both Arabic and English.

The dirham has been pegged to the US dollar since 1980, at a mid rate of $1 to Dhs.3.6725.

# People With Disabilities

In keeping with its philosophy of being 'the city that cares', Dubai is starting to consider the needs of disabled visitors more seriously. Dubai International Airport is well equipped for disabled travellers, with automatic doors, large lifts and all counters accessible by wheelchair users, as well as several services such as porters, special transportation and quick check-in to avoid long queues. Dubai Transport has a few specially modified taxis for journeys from the airport and

Essentials

Local Knowledge

around town. Most of Dubai's five-star hotels have wheelchair access, and newer places have specially adapted rooms for the disabled. In general, facilities for disabled guests are limited, particularly at tourist attractions. Wheelchair ramps are often really nothing more than delivery ramps and therefore have steep angles. When asking if a location has wheelchair access, make sure it really does – an escalator is considered 'wheelchair access' by some.

# Police

In an effort to better serve visitors, the Dubai Police launched the Department for Tourist Security. It acts as a liaison between you and the police, although in general officers are extremely helpful. They are calm and understanding, and speak a multitude of languages. The police website (www.dubaipolice.gov.ae) is easy to navigate, helpful, and has extensive information on policies and procedures. For assistance, call the toll free number (800 4438). In 2007, a new hotline number was launched for people suffering problems on the beach (04 203 6398). These could include sexual harassment or annoyance by quad bikes. For other emergency services call 999 for police or ambulance and 997 for fire.

# Public Toilets

You will find plenty of clean, modern toilets in the malls but the outside world is another story. There is a distinct lack of public bathrooms on shopping streets and facilities on open beaches tend to be pretty basic so you'd be well advised to take your own toilet paper.

## Emergency Services

| Al Wasl Hospital | 04 324 1111 | Hospital |
|---|---|---|
| Ambulance | 998 /999 | Emergency services |
| American Hospital | 04 336 7777 | Hospital |
| Department For Tourist Security | 800 4438 | Police services |
| Dubai Police Emergency | 999 | Emergency services |
| Dubai Police HQ | 04 229 2222 | Police services |
| Fire Department | 997 | Emergency services |
| Iranian Hospital | 04 344 0250 | Hospital |
| Life Pharmacy | 04 344 1122 | 24 hour pharmacy |
| Municipality Emergency Number | 04 223 2323 | Emergency services |
| Rashid Hospital | 04 337 4000 | Hospital |
| Welcare Hospital | 04 282 7788 | Hospital |

## Telephone & Internet

It is possible to buy temporary (three month) SIM cards for
your mobile phones that work on a pay-as-you go basis.
You can buy the package from Du online (www.du.ae) or at
its outlets in most malls. For Dhs.70 you get air time to the
value of Dhs.69, a travel kit including map and the option to
upgrade should you decide to stay in Dubai. International
text messages are charged at 90 fils. Etisalat's 'Ahlan' package
costs Dhs.90. This includes Dhs.35 credit, and an extra 30 day
grace period when you can receive calls. It is available from
the airport and malls. You can easily buy top-up cards for
both packages from supermarkets, newsagents and petrol
stations. Mobile phone numbers in the UAE begin with a
prefix of 050 or 055.

Wi-Fi is available in many hotel rooms. Most five-star accommodation also includes the use of a business centre (sometimes for a fee) where there are computers and internet access. Cafes around Dubai offer free Wi-Fi and current hotspots include More cafe (p.205), The Coffee Bean & Tea Leaf on Beach Road and cafes in Mall of the Emirates (p.162).

# Time

The UAE is four hours ahead of UCT (Universal Coordinated Time – formerly known as GMT). There is no altering of clocks for daylight saving in the summer, so when Europe and North America loses an hour, the time in the UAE stays the same.

Most offices and schools are closed on Fridays (the holy day) and Saturdays. This causes few problems for visitors but you might find shops don't open until later on Fridays.

# Tipping

Tipping practices are similar across hotels, restaurants and bars in Dubai. No matter how much or who you tip, the money gets shared with the other staff. Often if you give money to a specific person and they keep it, they can get into trouble. Many places now add a service charge onto the bill but no-one really knows if this actually goes to your server so many add a little extra. The usual amount to tip is 10%. Most restaurant bills in hotels should automatically come with 10% municipality tax and 10% service charge included, so check the bill carefully.

In a taxi it is standard to round up the fare to the nearest Dhs.5 but this is not compulsory.

Heritage Village

# Newspapers & Magazines

There are several English language newspapers in Dubai. You will see free copies of *7Days* on display. This daily tabloid contains international news alongside cinema listings and gossip. *Gulf News* (Dhs.3) is a broadsheet with a more serious slant and sections on property, classifieds and celebrity news in addition to current affairs. *Emirates Today* has been re-branded as *Emirates Business 24:7*, a business paper focussing on the UAE and international markets. The UK broadsheet, *The Times*, publishes an international edition, and is available daily for Dhs.7.

You can buy many of the major glossy magazines in Dubai, but if they're imported from the US or Europe, you can expect to pay twice the normal cover price. Alternatively, you can pick up the Middle East versions of popular titles including *Harper's Bazaar*, *Grazia*, *OK!* and *Hello!* where you'll find all the regular gossip and news, with extra from around the region. *Time Out Dubai* is the best place to find weekly listings for films, concerts, cultural one-offs, sporting events and nightlife information.

# Television

If you're in Dubai on holiday it's unlikely you'll want to waste time watching television. Most hotel rooms will have satellite or cable, broadcasting a mix of local stations (Arabic soap operas, talks shows and American sitcoms) and international channels. You'll find MTV, major news stations and some BBC programming, in addition to the standard hotel room information loop.

# Radio

You might not be able to hear cutting-edge music on the airwaves, but if you can stand the adverts, Dubai's radio is adequate. There are stations broadcasting in English, French, Hindi, Malayalam and Urdu and daily schedules can be found in newspapers.

The English language stations operate 24 hours a day. Despite the mainly British presenters, the music leans towards American chart fodder. Tune into Dubai 92 (92.0 FM), Radio 1 (99.3 FM), The Coast (103.2 FM) for music or Dubai Eye (103.8 FM) for speech and sport. All stations broadcast regular news and travel updates. You can pick up BBC World Service in English and Arabic (87.9 FM). The UK's Virgin Radio launched in 2008 and can be picked up on 104.4 FM.

# Books & Maps

If you want to read more about Dubai, the UAE and the Middle East region in general, there are plenty of books from which to choose. Explorer Publishing produces a range of regional activity guides, such as the *UAE Off-Road Explorer*, *Oman Off-Road Explorer* and the *Oman Trekking Explorer*. *The Dubai Red-Tape Explorer* and *Dubai Residents' Guide* are essential reading if you decide to settle in the city. For another perspective, Wilfred Thesiger's accounts of trekking across the Empy Quarter in the 1940s such as *Arabian Sands* and *Across the Empty Quarter* are fascinating.

*Dubai Mini Map* is a handy, pocket-sized map that will have you navigating the city like a local in no time. The *UAE Mini Map* will help you if you plan travel to the other emirates (p.103).

## Websites & Blogs

Despite the fact you might stumble across some truly ugly and unhelpful websites, the UAE is pretty switched on. Online listings, ticket booking, local news, the Yellow Pages and airport information are all available. Some sites are blocked on the grounds that their content is 'inconsistent with the religious, political, cultural and moral values of the UAE'.

In a mixed society it's no surprise lots of people have a lot on which to comment. Blogging is popular, despite occasional censorship. From long-time residents to newbie expats, it seems everyone has an opinion on their adopted city.

### Websites

| | |
|---|---|
| www.ameinfo.com | Middle East business news |
| www.dubaiairport.com | Airport information with weather forecast |
| www.dubaicityguide.com | Listings and events |
| www.dubaidutyfree.com | Dubai Duty Free |
| www.dubaipolice.gov.ae | Dubai Police information |
| www.dwtc.com/ directory.governme.htm | Embassies in Dubai |
| www.expatwoman.com | Information on living in Dubai from a woman's perspective |
| www.grapeshisha.com | Helpful info on visiting and living in Dubai |
| www.gulf-news.com | Dubai news |
| www.secretdubai.blogspot.com | Popular and controversial blog |
| www.timeoutdubai.com | Listings and tickets |
| www.yellowpages.ae | Yellow Pages online |

Dubai Marina

# Public Holidays

The Islamic calendar starts from the year 622AD, the year of Prophet Muhammad's migration (Hijra) from Mecca to Al Madinah. Hence the Islamic year is called the Hijri year and dates are followed by AH (AH stands for Anno Hegirae, meaning 'after the year of the Hijra'). As some holidays are based on the sighting of the moon and do not have fixed dates on the Hijri calendar, Islamic holidays are more often than not confirmed less than 24 hours in advance.

The main Muslim festivals are Eid Al Fitr (the festival of the breaking of the fast, which marks the end of Ramadan) and Eid Al Adha (the festival of the sacrifice, which marks the end of the pilgrimage to Mecca). Mawlid Al Nabee is the holiday celebrating the Prophet Muhammad's birthday, and Lailat Al Mi'raj celebrates the Prophet's ascension into heaven.

In general, public holidays have little bearing on daily life in Dubai with shops opening perhaps a bit later. During Ramadan however, food and beverages cannot be consumed in public during the day and smoking is prohibited. Women

| Public Holidays | |
|---|---|
| **Eid Al Adha (4 days) 2008** | Dec 9 (Moon) |
| **Eid Al Fitr (3 days) 2008** | Oct 2 (Moon) |
| **Islamic New Year's Day 2008** | Jan 10 (Moon) |
| **Lailat Al Mi'raj 2008** | Jul 31 (Moon) |
| **New Year's Day** | Jan 1 (Fixed) |
| **Prophet Muhammad's Birthday 2008** | Mar 20 (Moon) |
| **UAE National Day** | Dec 2 (Fixed) |

should dress more conservatively. You'll find nightlife dies
down for the month.

# Annual Events
Throughout the year the UAE hosts an impressive array of
events, from the world's richest horse race and international
tennis to well respected jazz and film festivals. Many attract
thousands of international visitors and tickets sell out quickly.

### Al Ain Aerobatic Show
January
Al Ain Airport                www.alainaerobaticshow.com
This five-day annual air show sees participation from flying
dare-devils from around the world. There is a spectator
grandstand for plane enthusiasts and those looking for a
fun day out. Both military and civilian planes take part in the
aerobatic displays. There is also a biennial airshow event in
Dubai (the next will be November 2009).

### Camel Racing
October to April
Nad Al Sheba
The sight of these ungainly animals is an extraordinary
spectacle, especially as racing camels can change hands for
as much as Dhs.10 million. This sport suffered a bit of bad
press due to the use of child jockeys, but that has all changed
with the introduction of robot camel replacements. Morning
races take place throughout the winter at the Nad Al Sheba
club and start very early; you need to be there by 07:00 as the
races are over by 08:30. Admission is free.

### Dubai International Film Festival

December

Various Locations

www.diff.ae

Having debuted in December 2004, this has become a hotly anticipated annual event and marks a real achievement for the UAE film industry. Premieres are generally held at Madinat Jumeirah, while screenings take place across the city. The festival brings together a good collection of Hollywood and international arthouse films, as well as work from the region.

### Dubai International Jazz Festival

March

Dubai Media City

www.chilloutproductions.com

Firmly established over the last few years, the Jazz Festival attracts a broad range of artists from all around the world to a chilled and pleasant setting in Dubai Media City. Courtney Pine, David Gray and Jamie Cullum have all featured.

### Dubai Rugby Sevens

December

Sports City

www.dubairugby7s.com

This three-day rugby event attracts more than 70,000 spectators over three days. With alcohol on sale at the stadium, the party atmosphere carries on until the small hours. Top international teams compete for the coveted 7s trophy while local teams from all over the Gulf try their luck.

### Dubai Shopping Festival

January to February

Various Locations

www.mydsf.com

A combination of a festival and a shopping extravaganza, Dubai Shopping Festival, or DSF as it is popularly known, is hard to miss. There are bargains galore in the participating outlets and spectacular fireworks each evening. It's a great (although rather congested) time to be in the city.

## Dubai Tennis Championships
February/March

Aviation Club    www.dubaitennischampionships.com

The $1,000,000 Dubai Tennis Championships is a great chance to see the top men's and women's seeds in an intimate setting. Firmly established on the ATP and WTP circuit, the tournament attracts the world's best. The women's tournament takes place in the first week, the men's during the second.

## Dubai World Cup
March

Nad Al Sheba    www.dubaiworldcup.com

The Dubai World Cup is billed as the richest horse race in the world: last year's total prize money was more than $15,000,000. The prize for the Group One Dubai World Cup race alone was a staggering $6,000,000. It is held on a Saturday to ensure maximum media coverage in the west. With a buzzing, vibrant atmosphere, it's also one of the year's big social occasions.

## UAE Desert Challenge
October & November

Jebel Ali Racecourse &
 Empty Quarter    www.uaedesertchallenge.com

This is the highest profile motorsport event in the country and is often the culmination of the World Championship in cross-country rallying. It attracts some of the world's top rally drivers and bike riders who compete in the car, truck and motocross categories.

# Getting Around

**It might be known for its tortuous traffic and stifling heat but don't let that put you off travelling around Dubai – it's easier than you think.**

You may have heard horror stories about arduous commutes, sticky strolls in the summer and terrifying taxi journeys but it is surprisingly simple, and pretty cheap, to get around Dubai. The metro system is hailed as the solution to carpark-like motorways but that won't be running until 2009. For now, taxis are the preferred method of transport, but don't overlook the cheap bus routes and a good walk during the cooler winter months. If you prefer to be in control then hiring a car is a great way to get out of the city but bear in mind the questionable driving of many motorists. If you're keen to get off the road then take a trip on a traditional abra or modern water taxi. Many people use them for daily trips and they offer a fresh perspective on the city.

## Bus

There are currently more than 60 bus routes through the main residential and commercial areas of Dubai, with the services available recently being clarified with a colour-coding system. While the buses are air-conditioned and modern they are rather crowded. Efforts are being made to display better timetables and route plans at bus stops and stations to encourage people to use buses. The main bus

Crossing the creek by abra

station is near the Gold Souk in Deira and in Bur Dubai on Al Ghubaiba Road near the Plaza Cinema. Buses run at regular intervals until midnight or so. Fares are cheap at between Dhs.1 and Dhs.3 per journey, and are paid to the driver when you board, so try to have the exact change ready. The Road and Transport Authority (RTA) call centre number is 800 9090 and its website (www.rta.ae) has comprehensive route plans, timetables and fares.

## Street Strife

To make navigation more confusing, places may not be referred to by their official name. For example, Al Jumeira Road is often known as Beach Road, and Interchange One on Sheikh Zayed Road is invariably called Defence Roundabout. You'll notice that certain streets around Dubai have been given the names of prominent Arab cities such as Cairo and Muscat. This followed a directive from Sheikh Hamdan bin Rashid Al Maktoum.

## Cycling

A lot of care is needed when cycling in the UAE as some drivers pay little attention to other cars, much less cyclists. Also, in the hotter months, you'll be peddling in 45ºC heat. If you are visiting in winter and want some outdoor exercise it might be best to head to Creekside Park (p.84) where you can rent a bike and explore in safety.

## Metro

There are currently no trains in the UAE, but work on the Dubai Metro transit system is already underway. It aims to be the largest driverless metro system in the world, and will be focused on two lines. The Red Line starts at Dubai airport and travels alongside Sheikh Zayed Road to the new developments in the south of the city and Jebel Ali, while the Green Line will service the city centre. Trains should be running by late 2009.

# Driving & Car Hire

It's a brave individual who gets behind the wheel in Dubai. Drivers are erratic, roads are constantly changing and the traffic jams can last for hours. On the bright side, most cars are automatic, which makes city driving a lot easier. Parking is free and plentiful at most malls and is cheap on street, although spaces can be at a premium. During the week traffic heading into Dubai from Deira in the morning and out in the evening is horrendous. Weekends, especially Fridays, are much clearer on the roads. You'll be driving on the right-hand side of the road. Be bold, use your indicators, expect the unexpected but anticipate the worst and you'll be fine.

## Car Rental Agencies

| Avis | 04 295 7121 | www.avisuae.com |
| --- | --- | --- |
| Budget Rent-a-Car | 04 295 6667 | www.budget-uae.com |
| Diamond Lease | 04 343 4330 | www.diamondlease.com |
| EuroStar Rent-a-Car | 04 266 1117 | www.eurostarrental.com |
| Hertz | 04 282 4422 | www.hertz-uae.com |
| National Car Rental | 04 283 2020 | www.national-me.com |
| Thrifty Car Rental | 800 4694 | www.thriftyuae.com |

International car rental companies, plus a few local firms, can be found in Dubai. Prices range from Dhs.80 a day for smaller cars to Dhs.1,000 for limousines. Comprehensive insurance is essential; make sure that it includes personal accident coverage.

To rent a car, you are required to produce a copy of your passport, a valid international driving licence and two photographs. The rental company may be able to help arrange international or temporary local licences for visitors.

# Taxi

If you don't rent a car, taxis are the most common way of getting around. There are seven companies operating more than 6,000 metered taxis with a fixed fare structure. All cars are clean and modern. A fleet of 'ladies' taxis', with distinctive pink roofs, was launched in 2007. These cars have female drivers and are meant for female passengers only. The pickup fare ranges from Dhs.3 to Dhs.7, depending on the time of day and taxi company. It is also possible to hire a taxi for 12 or 24 hour periods. Taxis can be flagged down by the side of the road or you can make a taxi booking through Dubai Transport by calling 04 208 0808.

To make life a little more confusing, taxi drivers occasionally lack any knowledge of the city and passengers may have to direct them. Be sure to carry a map or the phone number of your destination just in case.

# Walking

Cities in the UAE are generally very car oriented and not designed to encourage walking. Additionally, summer temperatures of more than 45°C are not conducive to strolling through the city. The winter months, however, make walking a pleasant way to explore. There aren't many pavements however, so you're best heading to places such as Al Dhiyafah Street (p.88), Plant Street (p.89) and Beach Road (p.151) for a stroll. There's also a running track along Jumeira Open Beach (p.79), starting from Dubai Marine Resort (www.dxbmarine.com), which is popular during the cooler months.

# Water Taxi

Opportunities for boat travel in the emirates are limited unless you take a dhow. Crossing the creek by abra is a common method of transport for many people living in Bur Dubai and Deira, with the number of passengers in 2006 estimated at nearly 26 million. Abra stations have been upgraded recently, while fares cost just Dhs.1. Another recent addition to the creek was a fleet of air-conditioned water buses. These operate on four different routes crossing the creek, with fares set at Dhs.4 per trip. A 'tourist' route also operates, with a 45 minute creek tour costing around Dhs.25 per person.

**Further Out**

If you want to explore the UAE during your stay then you'll need a driver or rental car. The East Coast (p.106) is known for its wonderful coastline and watersports, all easily accessible within a two hour drive. There are bus services to Abu Dhabi (p.103) that are cheap but basic. See www.rta.ae.

## Places To Stay

# The vast array of five-star hotels has given Dubai a reputation for luxurious breaks and flawless service, but there's a lot more besides.

In addition to a high number of plush hotels, Dubai has plenty of four, three, two and one-star places, and even a youth hostel. A new hotel seems to spring up every few months – 22,000 rooms are planned before the end of 2008. In true 'if you build it, they will come' style, room occupancy rates have soared over the last few years and currently stand at an annual average of 85% – one of the highest in the world.

Depending on the kind of holiday you want and, of course, your funds, you can choose from expensive deluxe suites or economical basic rooms. In general, prices are high so those on a budget might want to consider someone like www.mydubaistay.com for self-catering villas and apartments.

Most hotels are within 30 minutes of the airport and tend to be either on the beach, by the creek or on Sheikh Zayed Road. The coastal options will probably allow access to a private beach but if you're in Dubai on business then proximity to the financial areas of DIFC and Trade Centre is likely to be more important. If you are in town to shop then take your pick as malls are everywhere. With so many luxury hotels and resorts in Dubai, there's no reason why you can't combine a stay in a city centre hotel with a few nights at a desert resort, such as Bab Al Shams (p.47).

### Al Maha Desert Resort & Spa
www.al-maha.com
04 832 9900
Set within a 225 sq km conservation reserve, this stunning luxury getaway resembles a typical bedouin camp, but conditions are anything but basic. Each suite has its own private pool, and guests can enjoy fine dining on their own veranda.

### Bab Al Shams Desert Resort & Spa
www.babalshams.com
04 832 6699
This elegant desert resort in a traditional Arabic fort setting is home to the region's first open-air Arabic restaurant. Facilities include the luxurious Satori Spa, an infinity swimming pool and bar with breathtaking views over the dunes.

### Burj Al Arab
www.burj-al-arab.com
04 301 7777
Architecturally unique, the world's tallest hotel stands at 321 metres high on its own man-made island, and is dramatic, lavish and exclusive. Guests are looked after by a host of butlers. You will need to make a reservation if dining. Map 3 C1 🕄

### Crowne Plaza

www.crowneplaza.com
04 331 1111
Firm Sheikh Zayed Road favourite with
560 rooms. The complex has its own
shopping mall, a health club, as well as bars,
restaurants and cafes including Trader Vic's
(p.230), Wagamama, Harvesters and popular
nightclub Zinc (p.233). Map 7 D2 ◪

### InterContinental Dubai
### Festival City

www.ichotelsgroup.com
04 701 1111
Michelin-starred chef Pierre Gagnaire is
the star culinary attraction. The hotel has
extensive spa facilities and all of its rooms
and suites have a view of either Dubai Creek
or the Festival Marina. Map 6 C2 ◪

### Jumeirah Beach Hotel

www.jumeirah.com
04 348 0000
One of Dubai's landmarks. Built in the shape
of a wave with a dynamic and colourful
interior, the hotel has 618 rooms, all with
a sea view. It has a wide range of bars and
restaurants, including Villa Beach (p.238) and
360° (p.239). Map 3 C1 ◪

### Madinat Jumeirah
www.madinatjumeirah.com
04 366 8888
This resort has two hotels, Al Qasr and Mina A'Salam, with 940 luxurious rooms and suites, and exclusive summer houses, all linked by man-made waterways navigated by abras. Nestled between the two is Souk Madinat Jumeirah (p.165). Map 3 B1 🟨

### One&Only Royal Mirage
www.oneandonlyroyalmirage.com
04 399 9999
Blessed with an intimate atmosphere, this hotel features unparalleled service and dining, while a luxury spa treatment here is the ultimate indulgence. Try Moroccan cuisine at Tagine (p.201), or enjoy late nights at Kasbar (p.243). Map 2 E2 🟨

### The Palace – The Old Town
www.sofitel.com
04 428 7888
Situated close to Burj Dubai, The Palace boasts 242 deluxe rooms. There's butler service for all rooms, not to mention great views of the world's (current) tallest building. Its Asado (p.227) steak restaurant is highly recommended. Map 4 D3 🟨

**Essentials**

**Places To Stay**

### Park Hyatt Dubai
www.dubai.park.hyatt.com
04 602 1234
Mediterranean and Moorish in style with low buildings and natural colours, Park Hyatt has 225 rooms, each with a balcony or terrace with great views. Enjoys a prime waterfront location next to Dubai Creek Golf & Yacht Club (p.125). Map 5 C4 **10**

### Raffles Dubai
www.raffles.com
04 324 8888
Raffles has 248 guest rooms and suites and the Raffles Amrita Spa with a unique rooftop garden: an oasis of exotic flowers and orchids around a pool. There's nine restaurants and bars; China Moon (p.219) is already a hot nightspot. Map 5 B4 **11**

### Shangri-La Hotel
www.shangri-la.com
04 343 8888
This 43 storey hotel on Sheikh Zayed Road offers fantastic views of the coast and the city. There are 301 guest rooms and suites, a health club and spa, two swimming pools and a variety of restaurants and bars, including Marrakesh. Map 7 A2 **12**

# Hostels & Guesthouses

Five-star finery is not for everyone. Guesthouses may lack the facilities of the big hotels but will offer more personal service and often a more intimate stay. La Maison d'Hôtes (04 344 1838, www.lamaisondhotesdubai.com), near the beach in Jumeira, is a stunning collection of 20 guest rooms in three villas. Elegantly decorated in French style, there is a restaurant (unlicensed), two swimming pools, and a gym. For a slightly more basic B&B, Fusion (www.fusionhotels.com) is a good choice. Situated in an Arabian villa, it offers gardens and pools, friendly staff and complimentary breakfasts.

The XVA Gallery (p.61) is an authentic, artistic and inspired guesthouse in Bastakiya. There are uniquely designed rooms, an open courtyard and permanent exhibitions on offer.

Dubai Youth Hostel (04 298 8161) provides the cheapest accommodation in town. You'll find it in Al Nahda Road near Al Mulla Plaza in the north of the city. There are more than 50 beds available for Dhs.80 per night (YHA members) or Dhs.95 (non-members), including breakfast, in one of 20 very clean, two-bed dormitory rooms. Double rooms are Dhs.230 for non-members (Dhs.200 for members), including breakfast. Check-in is always open.

Hotel apartments and villas, which offer more homely accommodation and the benefit of regular cleaning and other facilities, are a good option for short and extended stays. The website www.mydubaistay.com is a good resource, listing available apartments and villas across the city, with a cost comparison chart and online reservation facility.

# Exploring

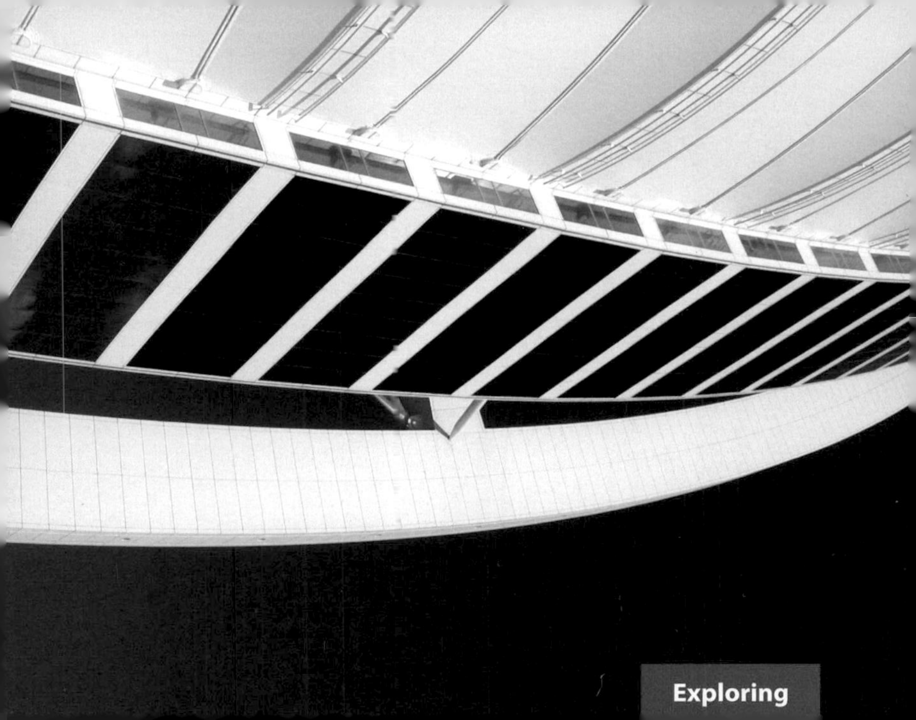

# Exploring

# Explore Dubai

## From expansive deserts to massive malls, Dubai is a city of superlatives that will impress even the most seasoned traveller.

Dubai provides a wealth of contrasting images: Ferraris parked outside falafel shops, massive skyscrapers shading pristine mosques, billionaires, cranes, camels, palaces and windtowers. The city is filled with luxurious five-star hotels and huge shopping malls, it has some of the top nightspots in the Middle East, as well as several museums, heritage sites and places of cultural interest. Quite a mix.

Don't let the severe traffic and ever-expanding footprint disorient you – the city itself is fairly easy to navigate. It is split in half by Dubai Creek, the lifeline of the city. The 15km long, 500m wide body of water separates Deira (p.64) in the north and Bur Dubai (p.58) in the south. The two sides are connected by five main crossing points: Al Shindagha Tunnel, Maktoum Bridge, Garhoud Bridge, Floating Bridge and Business Bay Bridge. For a more traditional way of crossing, join the many residents who still use the wooden abras or water taxis (p.45).

On the Bur Dubai side, you'll find the slow-paced leisure of Oud Metha and Umm Hurair (p.84) and people-watching of Satwa (p.88) and Karama (p.58). There are also the glamorous, beach-filled areas of Jumeira (p.78) and Umm Suqeim (p.96) along the coast. Trade Centre, the area surrounding the

The bright lights of Deira

skyscraper-lined Sheikh Zayed Road (p.92), also lies on this side of the creek. On the Deira side, you'll find Garhoud (p.74), which will inevitably rise in popularity with the completion of shopping and entertainment hub, Dubai Festival City (p.159). Check out the inside front cover map to see the boundaries of each area.

Each heading in this chapter has both a map reference and small highlighted number, which denotes its exact location on the maps (p.268). Each exploring area corresponds to the areas in the Going Out section too (p.172), so you won't have to worry about where to find a falafel or stiff drink after bashing some dunes (p.128) or wandering the alleys of Bastakiya (p.58).

# Heritage Sites

# Museums & Art Galleries

# Parks

At A Glance

Exploring

## Bur Dubai & Karama

**Amateur historians and budget gourmands will love Bur Dubai's museums and heritage sites and Karama's cheap eateries.**

What was once just a flat, sandy space with a sprinkling of palm trees and barasti (palm) houses is now the bustling heart of the city. It may not be the commercial centre that it once was, but for exploring, this is one of the best spots in Dubai. Of particular note is the enchanting Bastakiya area, which offers authentic, historical sites worth investigating, as well as Dubai Museum (p.59), the souks and Bur Dubai Corniche. *For restaurants and bars in the area, see p.182. For shopping, see BurJuman (p.157) and Karama (p.148).*

### Bastakiya

Between Diwan Roundabout & Al Faheidi Roundabout

The Bastakiya area is one of the oldest heritage sites in Dubai and certainly one of the most atmospheric. The neighbourhood dates back to the early 1900s when traders from the Bastak area of southern Iran were encouraged to settle there by tax concessions granted by Sheikh Maktoum bin Hashar, the ruler of Dubai at the time. The area is characterised by traditional windtower houses, built around courtyards and clustered together around a winding maze of alleyways. The distinctive four-sided windtowers (barjeel), seen on top of the traditional flat-roofed buildings, were an early form of air conditioning. Map 5 C1 ◼

### Dubai Museum
Near Bastakiya

04 353 1862
www.dubaitourism.ae

Located in Al Fahedi Fort, which dates back to 1787, this museum is creative and well thought-out. All parts of life from Dubai's past are represented in an attractive and interesting way; walk through a souk from the 1950s, stroll through an oasis, see into a traditional house, get up close to local wildlife, learn about the archaeological finds or go 'underwater' to discover pearl diving and fishing industries. There are some entertaining mannequins to pose with too. Entry costs Dhs.3 for adults and Dhs.1 for children under 6 years old. Open daily 08:30 to 20:30 (14:30 to 20:30 on Fridays). Map 5 C1 ◻

### Heritage & Diving Village
Near Al Shindagha Tunnel

04 393 7151
www.dubaitourism.ae

Located near the mouth of Dubai Creek, the Heritage & Diving Village focuses on Dubai's maritime past, pearl diving traditions and architecture. Visitors can observe traditional potters and weavers practising their craft the way it has been done for centuries. Local women serve traditionally cooked snacks – one of the rare opportunities you'll have to sample genuine Emirati cuisine. Camel rides are also available most afternoons and evenings. The Village is particularly lively during the Dubai Shopping Festival (p.38) and Eid celebrations, with performances including traditional sword dancing. Open daily 08:30 to 22:30. Map 5 C1 ◼

### The Majlis Gallery

04 353 6233

Al Faheidi Street

www.majlisgallery.com

The Majlis Gallery is a converted Arabic house, complete with windtowers and courtyard. Small, whitewashed rooms lead off the central garden and host exhibitions by contemporary artists. In addition to the fine art collection, there's an extensive range of hand-made glass, pottery, fabrics, frames, and unusual furniture. The gallery hosts exhibitions throughout the year, but is worth visiting at any time. Open Saturday to Thursday 09:30 to 20:00  Map 5 C1 ◳

### Sheikh Mohammed Centre for Cultural Understanding

04 353 6666

Bastakiya

www.cultures.ae

This facility was established to help visitors and residents understand the customs and traditions of the UAE. It organises tours in Jumeira Mosque (p.80), a walking tour of the Bastakiya area, and weekly coffee mornings where UAE nationals explain the Emirati way of life. The centre is worth a look for the majlis-style rooms around the courtyard and great views through the palm trees and windtowers. Open Sunday to Thursday 08:00 to 15:00 and 09:00 to 13:00 on Saturday.  Map 5 C1 ❶

### Sheikh Saeed Al Maktoum's House

04 393 7139

Next to Heritage Village, Al Shindagha   www.dubaitourism.ae

Dating from 1896, this carefully restored house-turned-museum is built in the traditional manner of the Gulf coast, using coral covered in lime and sand-coloured plaster. The interesting displays in many rooms show rare and wonderful photographs of all aspects of life in Dubai pre-oil. There is also an old currency and stamp collection, and great views over the creek from the upper floor. Entry is Dhs.2 for adults, Dhs.1 for children and free for children under 6 years old. Map 5 C1 🖪

## XVA Gallery

Bastakiya

04 353 5383

www.xvagallery.com

Located in the centre of the maze-like alleyways of Bastakiya, this is one of Dubai's most interesting art galleries. Originally a windtower house, it's worth a visit for its architecture alone. The gallery focuses on paintings, sculpture and art installations and hosts many exhibitions from local and international artists throughout the year. There are eight guest rooms located on the upper floors, where you can chill out in rocking chairs and gaze over the minarets to Bur Dubai. Open Saturday to Thursday 09:00 to 19:00 and Friday 10:00 to 17:00. Map 5 C1 🖪

# Karama

Primarily a residential area, consisting of relatively low-cost flats in low-rise apartment blocks, Karama is well known for having something for everyone. It also has a great shopping area, the popular Karama Shopping Complex (p.148). Karama's merchants are a far cry from their mall counterparts and offer a worthwhile challenge if you like practising your haggling skills. There's a great range of inexpensive restaurants serving tasty cuisine from Arabic and Indian to Sri Lankan and Singaporean, including Chef Lanka (p.185), Karachi Darbar (p.186) and Aryaas (p.183).

If you only do one thing in...
# Bur Dubai & Karama

Get schooled at the informative Dubai Museum (p.59). Learn about life in Dubai 50 years ago to really appreciate how much has changed.

## Best for...

**Eating:** Take a break from the glitzy hotel restaurants and taste some authentic Pakistani cuisine at Karachi Darbar (p.186).

**Sightseeing:** The winding alleyways of Bastakiya (p.58) will linger in the memory long after you leave Dubai.

**Shopping:** It's a tough call, but cheap, cheerful Karama (p.148) wins out over the designer chic of BurJuman (p.157).

**Relaxation:** Duck into tranquility at The Majlis Gallery (p.60) or XVA (p.61).

**Families:** Let the kids hop on a camel while you gorge on freshly baked bread, all in the midst of living history at the Heritage & Diving Village (p.59).

Traditional Arabian architecture

Bur Dubai & Karama

# Deira

**Deira's busy creekside streets capture the essence of old Dubai far better than any museum.**

Deira used to be the residential hub of Dubai, and is still an incredibly atmospheric area. Narrow convoluted streets bustle with activity while gold, spices, perfumes and general goods are touted in numerous souks. The streets are full of people, especially in the evenings. As the oldest part of the city, there is plenty of heritage around, and while it can be a crazy place to navigate by car, you can avoid the frustrations of the snarled-up traffic if you visit at quieter times of the day.

Another cultural attraction is Dubai's largest and busiest fish market (near the Hyatt Regency Hotel), where you can stock up on the freshest seafood in town at bargain prices. You can pay a 'wheelbarrow man' to follow you and carry your shopping, and someone else to gut your fish. A fish museum has recently been created at Deira Fish Market to give shoppers and tourists more information about the 350 species in the Arabian Gulf, and the history of the fishing trade in the UAE.

If it's rugs you want then Deira Tower on Al Nasr Square is worth a visit. About 40 shops offer a colourful profusion of carpets from Iran, Pakistan, Turkey and Afghanistan to suit everyone's taste and pocket.

For **restaurants and bars** in the area, see p.188. For **shopping**, see Deira City Centre (p.158) and souks (p.152).

Clocktower Roundabout

## Al Ahmadiya School & Heritage House   04 226 0286

Al Khor Street, Al Ras   www.dubaitourism.ae

Established in 1912 for Dubai's elite, Al Ahmadiya School was the earliest regular school in the city. A visit here is an excellent opportunity to see the history of education in the UAE. Situated in what is becoming a small centre for heritage (Al Souk Al Khabeer), it is an interesting example of a traditional Emirati family home, which dates back to 1890. Admission to both is free. Open Saturday to Thursday 08:00 to 19:30 and 15:00 to 19:30 on Friday. Map 5 C1 ⑥

## Al Mamzar Beach Park   04 296 6201

Near Hamriya Port, Al Hamriya   www.dm.gov.ae

With its four clean beaches, open spaces and plenty of greenery, Al Mamzar is a popular spot. The well-maintained beaches have sheltered areas for swimming and changing rooms with showers. Air-conditioned chalets, with barbecues, can be rented on a daily basis, costing from Dhs.150 to Dhs.200. There are two swimming pools with lifeguards on duty. Entrance is Dhs.5 per person or Dhs.30 per car (including all occupants). Map 1 F1

## Al Riqqa Road

Deira

Al Riqqa Road is one of the central thoroughfares of Deira. The restaurants, shops and cafes and wide pavements are scattered with alfresco diners in the winter. This is the perfect example of a Dubai neighbourhood that has changed little in the past 15 years and is well worth exploring. Map 5 D3 ⑧

**Magic Planet**　　　　　　　　　　04 295 4333
Deira City Centre　　　　　　　www.deiracitycentre.com
This blaring, boisterous play area is a hugely popular
destination for kids accompanying their mums and dads
on long shopping trips. There are various rides, including
bumper cars, and the latest video games. Entrance is free, and
you use the facilities on a 'pay as you play' basis.  Map 5 D4 **10**

# The Creek
The first settlements in the area were positioned at the
mouth of Dubai Creek. Later, it was dredged and lengthened,
enabling maritime commerce. No visitor should leave without
experiencing a trip across the water on a commuter abra (p.45)
for Dhs.1, or a tourist abra.

　　Both sides of the creek are lined by corniches that come
alive in the evenings as residents head out for a stroll and
traders take stock. Take a stroll along the dhow wharfage
where wooden dhows lazily docked by the water's edge,
tightly packed with everything from fruit and vegetables to
televisions and maybe even a car or two, are unloaded.

　　Take the pedestrain underpass to the left of the abra station
to enter the oldest market in Dubai, which now sells mainly
household items. Nearby is the Spice Souk (p.154), where the
aroma of saffron and cumin fill the air. The streets between Al
Nasr Square and the Gold Souk (p.153) are filled with shops
shimmering with white gold and platinum.

　　Some of the finest alfresco dining can be found overlooking
the creek traffic. QD's (p.210) offers shisha and drinks, while
The Terrace (p.210) is a stylish bar.

Exploring

# If you only do one thing in...
# Deira

Watch the dhows unload at the corniche, then head for a stroll around Dubai's famous souks.

## Best for...

**Eating:** Hop on a dhow for a delicious dinner cruise (p.181). This is by far the best way to get your fill of food, facts, and photographs.

**Sightseeing:** Reserve a table at the Hyatt Regency's Al Dawaar (p.191). The city's only revolving restaurant offers fantastic views of the creek and beyond.

**Shopping:** Stroll through the glittering streets of the Gold Souk (p.153) before following your nose to the Spice Souk (p.154).

**Relaxation:** Step into the calm courtyard of the Al Ahmadiya School & Heritage House (p.64), where you'll find some quiet in the Deira storm.

**Families:** Leave the traffic-filled bridges and take the kids across the creek by abra.

Clockwise from top left: An Abra on Dubai Creek, Dhow details, Spice Souk, Al Ahmadiya School & Heritage House

# Dubai Marina & Al Sufouh

With a new tower rising from the sand almost daily, this ode to construction and luxury is the heart of New Dubai, offering shopping and dining galore.

Previously home to just a handful of waterfront hotels, the Marina (or Marsa Dubai to use its proper title) has seen some of Dubai's most intensive construction in recent years. Apartment buildings are popping up along every inch of the man-made marina, and a drive past the area is a testament to just how quickly this city is expanding. The coast is home to a number of five-star hotels, such as Jumeirah Beach Hotel (p.49) and One&Only Royal Mirage (p.48). Al Sufouh is the base for three business and academic hubs: Media City, Internet City and Knowledge Village, but also has isolated clusters of villas and a peaceful air. Before too long though there will be a few new neighbours moving in, as soon the famous Palm Jumeirah opens fully to residents. Visitors wanting to get up close to this modern marvel can walk or drive onto the trunk of the palm, but for the best views try a helicopter ride (p.112). For *restaurants and bars* in the area, see p.196. For *shopping, head to Marina Market (p.155).*

## Jumeirah Beach Residence

Dubai Marina

At the epicentre of the New Dubai construction lies this massive, 40 tower development. It's a good base for exploring the nearby hotels and public beach. A few restaurants and shops have already opened within the devleopment, including Frankie's (p.198). The real reason for exploring this area, however, is to experience the largest, single-phase residential development in the world.  Map 2 C1 **11**

## Marina Walk
Dubai Marina

The area around Dubai Marina Towers was the first to be developed, back in 1998. It is one of the most desirable addresses in the city, with close proximity to good restaurants and stunning views of the marina and the Arabian Gulf beyond. Marina Walk, the boulevard at the base of the towers, is home to a number of independent restaurants and cafes such as popular shisha spot, Chandelier (p.197). It is a great place for a stroll any time but it really comes to life in the evenings and cooler months when you can sit and gaze out across the gleaming yachts and the flashing lights of high-rise hotels and apartments.  Map 2 D2 **12**

## Marina Market
Dubai Marina                                www.marinamarket.ae

Open on Fridays and Saturdays, from October to April, Marina Market actively supports Dubai's budding artisan scene. The 50 stalls sell everything from wall art and photography to handmade jewellery and clothing. Even if shopping isn't your thing, it's a good place to observe the 'Marina set' in their natural habitat while kicking back with a coffee or some shisha at a nearby cafe.  Map 2 D2 **12**

If you only do one thing in...

# Dubai Marina & Al Sufouh

Cruise past all the New Dubai construction on Sheikh Zayed Road. It's the best way to catch a glimpse of this city's future.

## Best for...

**Drinking:** Rooftop Lounge (p.203) at the One&Only Royal Mirage offers a sophisticated starlit night.

**Shopping:** Stroll through the refined culture of the Marina Market (p.71) and pick up some works by Dubai's emerging designers and artisans.

**Sightseeing:** The views from Marina Walk (p.71) change almost daily. Try to count the cranes.

**Relaxation:** Get the full body scrub at the Oriental Hammam (p.138) in the One&Only Royal Mirage.

**Eating:** Enjoy some pasta and a bottle of red, while listening to the pianist at Frankie's (p.198).

# Garhoud

## Already popular with tourists and locals, Garhoud's nightlife and shopping gets better by the day.

Between the creek and Deira lies the mostly residential area of Garhoud. With the exception of the relatively new Dubai Festival City, Garhoud comes alive after the sun has set and the traffic has subsided.

Entertainment seekers flock to the Irish Village (p.210), Century Village and Aviation Club each night to dine alfresco, drink and socialise. Dubai Festival City will soon boost Garhoud's popularity further – when it's completed it will be an entertainment hotspot with its three major hotels and creekside promenade. *For **restaurants and bars** in the area, see p.204. For **shopping**, see Dubai Festival City p.159.*

### Aviation Club
Near Garhoud Bridge

04 282 4122
www.aviationclub.ae

Mention Garhoud to any newcomer and they might shrug; mention the Irish Village and they'll offer a knowing smile. Thanks to its combination of live music, lakeside views and lots of booze, the Irish Village and neighbouring Century Village are perennially popular, due in no small part to their laidback vibe. Both belong to the much larger Aviation Club. It is also home to the tennis stadium and Akuru Spa (p.135), which is a fantastic spot for a wide variety of treatments at reasonable prices. Map 6 C1 14

Park Hyatt on Dubai Creek

### Dubai Creek Golf & Yacht Club
Opposite Deira City Centre Mall

04 295 6000
www.dubaigolf.com

This club has several bars and restaurants, but Boardwalk (p.206) is known for its memorable views. Grab a table outside in the cooler months. Within the grounds of the golf club lies the Park Hyatt Hotel (p.50). The hotel's range of restaurants, including The Thai Kitchen (p.208), sit by the creek.  Map 5 C4 **15**

### Dubai Festival City
Near Garhoud Bridge

04 213 6213
www.dubaifestivalcity.com

Dubai Festival City offers visitors plenty of distractions. The beautiful mall is large enough to spend a day in and has several worthy restaurants. The recently completed InterContinental (p.48) and Crown Plaza each house several decent eateries, including Anise (p.205). Best of all, there's a creekside walkway connecting all the buildings. For more details, see p.159.  Map 6 C2 **16**

# If you only do one thing in...
# Garhoud

Spend an afternoon, evening, or whole day at the Irish Village (p.210). Not just another theme pub, this is a Dubai institution.

## Best for...

**Drinking:** The Terrace (p.210) has a drinks list to match its stunning creekside setting.

**Sightseeing:** The creekside views from Boardwalk (p.206) are some of the best in the city.

**Shopping:** The spacious, well-designed halls of Festival City (p.159) offer a welcome respite from its often hectic big brothers.

**Relaxation:** Indulge yourself with a treatment at the highly rated Amara Spa at the Park Hyatt Hotel (p.135).

**Eating:** Alfresco dining options abound at the creekside walkway at Dubai Festival City (p.75).

# Jumeira's beaches, boutiques and art galleries offer a pleasant retreat from the city's bustling core.

Jumeira might not have the exotic atmosphere or history of Deira, but its beaches, shopping centres and pleasant, wide roads make up for it. That's not to say it doesn't have any culture. Jumeira Mosque (p.80) is one of the most recognisable places of worship in the city and welcomes tourists with tours and educational programmes, while the galleries will keep art enthusiasts happy.

Jumeira is one of the most desirable addresses for well-off expats and home to the infamous, coiffeured 'Jumeira Janes'. The popular Jumeira Open Beach (p.79) has showers and lifeguards, but unfortunately attracts a few voyeurs, so you may prefer to try the more private Jumeira Beach Park (p.79). *For **restaurants and bars** in the area see p.212. For **shopping**, see Mercato (p.164) and Beach Road (p.151).*

### Creative Art Centre
04 344 4394

Near Choithram
www.arabian-arts.com

A large gallery and shop with eight showrooms set in two villas, the Creative Art Centre has a wide range of original art, framed maps, and Arabian antiques and gifts. The selection of antiquities includes Omani chests and old doors. There's also a good selection of old weapons and silver. Lynda Shephard, the managing partner, is a well-known artist in both Oman and Dubai, and some of her works can be purchased here. The gallery also offers a picture-framing service. Map 4 B2 **16**

## Green Art Gallery

04 344 9888

Villa 23, St 51, behind Dubai Zoo    www.gagallery.com

Housed in an attractive single-storey villa, the Green Art Gallery features original art, limited-edition prints and hand-crafted work by artists from all over the world. In particular, the gallery draws on those influenced by the Arab world and its people. With large white minimalist walls and lots of floor space, Green Art makes a great stop-off if you fancy some peace and quiet and a little culture. Seasonal exhibitions are held from October to May. Map 4 E1 **17**

## Jumeira Beach Park

04 349 2555

Beach Road    www.dm.gov.ae

You get the best of both worlds here with plenty of grassy areas and vast expanses of beach. The facilities include sunlounger and parasol hire, lifeguards, toilets, showers, snack bar, play park and barbecue pits. Entry is Dhs.5 per person or Dhs.20 per car, including all occupants. Mondays are for women and children only. Open daily from 07:00, closing at 22:30 Sunday to Wednesday, and at 23:00 Thursday to Saturday and on holidays. Map 4 B1 **18**

## Jumeira Open Beach

Near Dubai Marine Beach Resort & Spa

One of the most popular free beaches in the city, this clean area offers both showers and lifeguards. Unfortunately, men staring at the sunbathing women can often be found loitering in the area. They may make the scene uncomfortable, but they mean no harm. A sprung running and bike track runs the length of the beach. Map 4 E1 19

### Jumeira Mosque
04 353 6666

Beach Road
smccu@eim.ae

This is easily the most beautiful mosque in the city and perhaps the best known. It is especially breathtaking at night when lit. Non-Muslims are not usually permitted entry to a mosque, but the Sheikh Mohammed Centre for Cultural Understanding (p.60) organises weekly tours (Saturday, Sunday, Tuesday and Thursday mornings at 10:00). Visitors are guided around the mosque and told all about the building, and then the hosts give a talk on Islam and the prayer ritual. You must dress conservatively – no shorts and no sleeveless tops. Women must also cover their hair with a head scarf or shawl, and all visitors will be asked to remove their shoes. Cameras are allowed and large groups can book private tours. Map 4 F1 20

### Majlis Ghorfat Um Al Sheef
04 394 6343

Beach Road
www.dubaitourism.co.ae

Constructed in 1955 from coral stone and gypsum, this simple building was used by the late Sheikh Rashid bin Saeed Al Maktoum as a summer residence. The ground floor is an open veranda (leewan or rewaaq), while upstairs the majlis (meeting place) is decorated with carpets, cushions, lanterns and rifles. The site has a traditional falaj irrigation system to direct water from a well, and in another corner there's a

Jumeira Mosque

barasti shelter constructed from palm branches and leaves. The Majlis is located just inland from Beach Road on Street 17, beside HSBC bank. Entry is Dhs.1 for adults and free for children under 6 years old.  Map 4 B1 **21**

## Safa Park

04 349 2111

Near Union Co-op & Choithrams, Al Wasl          www.dm.gov.ae

This huge, artistically divided park is a great place to escape the commotion of nearby Sheikh Zayed Road. Its many sports fields, barbecue sites and play areas make it one of the few places where locals and expats come together. Tuesday is ladies' day, but there is also a permanent ladies' garden within the park. Entry costs Dhs.3 (free for children under 3 years old). There's a great running track around the park's perimeter.  Map 4 B2 **22**

# If you only do one thing in...
# Jumeira

Take a tour of the most beautiful mosque in the city, and one of the few in the UAE open to non-Muslims (p.80).

## Best for...

**Outdoors:** Head to Jumeira Beach Park (p.79), rent a sunbed and parasol and experience the Dubai you've seen in the brochures.

**Families:** Give your kids a break from the sightseeing and let them run wild at Fun City in Mercato (p.164).

**Shopping:** Enjoy a wander through the malls and thriving independent fashion boutiques that line Beach Road (p.151).

**Relaxation:** Feel like a 'Jumeira Jane' by slipping into Elche spa for a treatment (p.135).

**Culture:** Witness the emerging Gulf art scene at the Green Art Gallery (p.79).

Clockwise from top: Jumeira Beach Park, Majlis Ghorfat Um Al Sheef, Mercato

# Oud Metha & Umm Hurair

**Although it was once known as the leisure capital of the city, people now flock to this area for luxury shopping and lazy afternoons.**

Oud Metha and Umm Hurair are in the centre of Dubai next to Karama, and bordered by the creek to the north. Wafi Mall (p.167) in Umm Hurair and Lamcy Plaza (p.161) in Oud Metha are popular shopping spots for both bargains and international fashion labels. The addition of Raffles Dubai (p.50) has improved the area's already impressive restaurant and bar roster. You'll also find some of the city's best leisure options including Creekside Park (below), Al Nasr Leisureland (p.85) and Wonderland Theme & Water Park (p.85).
*For restaurants and bars in the area, see p.216. For shopping, see Lamcy Plaza (p.161) and Wafi Mall (p.167).*

## Creekside Park

04 336 7633

Near Wonderland Theme & Water Park    www.dm.gov.ae

It may be in the heart of the city but Creekside Park is blessed with acres of gardens, fishing piers, jogging tracks, barbecue sites, children's play areas, restaurants and kiosks. There's also a mini falaj for irrigation and a large amphitheatre. Running along the park's 2.5km stretch of creek frontage is a cable car system, allowing visitors an unrestricted view from 30m in the air. From Gate Two, four-wheel cycles can be hired for Dhs.20 per hour. Admission costs Dhs.5. Map 5 C4 **23**

## Al Nasr Leisureland

04 337 1234

Opposite Mövenpick  www.alnasrleisureland.ae

Opened way back in 1979, this is the nearest Dubai gets to an old-school leisure park. With an ice-skating rink, bowling alley and arcade games, it is every teenager's dream – and parent's nightmare. But with tennis courts, a gym and regular indoor football, there's no doubt that Al Nasr is a great facility. There are also bumper cars and a mini rollercoaster. Map 5 B3 **24**

## Encounter Zone

04 324 7747

Wafi City  www.waficity.com

With a range of activities for all ages, Encounter Zone is a great stop-off to reward your kids after a day of shopping in Wafi Mall (p.167). Galactica is for teenagers and adults and features an inline skating and skateboarding park. Lunarland is for kids aged 1 to 8, and includes a small soft-play area for very tiny tots. Prices range from Dhs.5 to Dhs.25, or you can buy a day-pass for Dhs.15. Open from 10:00 to 22:00 Saturday to Tuesday, from 10:00 to 23:00 Wednesday and Thursday, and from 13:00 to 22:00 on Fridays. Map 5 B4 **25**

## Wonderland Theme & Water Park

04 324 1222

Near Creekside Park  www.wonderlanduae.com

Dubailand (p.265) may be lurking in the distance, but for now Wonderland remains Dubai's only theme park. Combining amusements and a water park, Wonderland will keep even the most distracted teenager in check with trampolines, video games, go-karting and paintballing. Opening hours are seasonal so check the website. Map 5 C4 **26**

MAKE UP FOR EVE

# If you only do one thing in...
# Oud Metha & Umm Hurair

Sample the joys of shopping, spas and oversized cocktails all under one roof at Wafi City (p.167).

## Best for...

**Eating:** There are top restaurants at Wafi Pyramids, but the modern Indian cuisine of Asha's (p.217) truly captures the imagination.

**Sightseeing:** Squeeze into a cable car in Creekside Park (p.84) for great views over the creek.

**Family:** Let the children loose at Encounter Zone (p.85). It's one of the few kids' zones that adults get a kick out of.

**Outdoors:** Get active at Wonderland Theme & Water Park (p.85) with slides, trampolines and more.

**Drinking:** Ginseng (p.219) has happy hour every day and one of the best cocktail lists in the city.

Clockwise from top: Raffles, Wafi Mall, Girseng

Oud Metha & Umm Hurair

# Satwa

## The pavement cafes, neon lights and constant buzz of Satwa make for some of Dubai's best people-watching.

Wedged between Jumeira and the Trade Centre, Satwa is an area of contrasts. At one end, quiet suburban streets boast smart villas, while a 15 minute walk will take you to Al Dhiyafah Street and Satwa Road, bustling thoroughfares lined with shops (the area is well known for its good-quality tailors) and plenty of inexpensive restaurants and cafes.

The Lebanese, Iranian and Pakistani eateries are some of the best in town, thanks to the diverse population of the area. When the weather is cool enough, it's a great place to wander around – the evenings get particularly busy, and Al Dhiyafah Street becomes a moving showroom of expensive, customised cars. *For **restaurants and bars** in the area, see p.222. For **shopping,** see Al Dhiyafah Street (p.88) and Plant Street (p.89).*

### Al Dhiyafah Street

Satwa

During the day, the wide, palm-lined Al Dhiyafah looks like any other street in the older sections of Dubai. Come night, however, it becomes a beacon for the post-club crowd with its many restaurants often filled until 05:00. Two of the most popular spots for a late-night feed are Al Mallah (p.223) and Ravi's (p.224). Sit at a pavement cafe and watch some of the most pimped out cars in Dubai cruise past. Map 4 F1 **27**

## Plant Street

Between Satwa Road & Al Wasl Road

Famous for pots and plants, pet shops, fabric shops and hardware outlets, Plant Street is another spot that hasn't changed much since the beginning of Dubai's boom. Head here on a Saturday evening to soak up the atmosphere, but women are advised to cover up unless they want to be stared at themselves.  Map 4 F1 28

## Satwa Park

Behind Al Moosa Towers                                    www.dm.gov.ae

This new community park opened its gates in 2006, and while certainly not on the scale of Safa or Zabeel parks, it does offer some welcome relief and relaxation in the shadows of the SZR skyscrapers. The park has tennis and basketball courts, a grass football pitch, and a running track around its perimeter. There's plenty of shade, seating, and grassy areas, and the kids' play area has the usual array of colourful slides and climbing frames.  Map 4 E2 29

## Iranian Mosque

Al Wasl Road

Non-Muslims can't enter the Iranian Mosque, but it's still worth admiring (and photographing) from the outside. The blue mosaic tiling, pillars, arches and elaborate minarets are typical of Persian architecture, making this one of the most photogenic sights in Dubai. The mosque also serves as a stunning counterpoint to some of the modern places of worship you'll see elsewhere in the city.  Map 4 F1 30

# If you only do one thing in...
## Satwa

Find a design, buy some fabric and take a stroll to the tailors (p.173) to get your dream garb for pennies.

## Best for...

**Eating:** Gorge yourself on a late-night curry feast at Ravi's (p.224).

**Outdoor:** Find a patch of grass under a tree at Satwa Park (p.89) and watch the shadows of Sheikh Zayed Road skyscrapers move with the setting sun.

**Sightseeing:** Take in the intricate tiled beauty of the Iranian Hospital and mosque (p.89) on Al Wasl Road.

**Culture:** Get a taste of what Dubai used to be like by taking a walk along Plant Street (p.89).

**Also In The Area:** Satwa is one of those places that's full of entertaining subtleties. Join a game of basketball at the courts near Rydges Plaza hotel, catch the match at the rowdy Boston Bar (p.225), or just find a bench and practice your people-watching.

Clockwise from top: Al Mallah, windtowers and Emirates Towers, the Iranian Mosque

# Sheikh Zayed Road

**From the Dubai World Trade Centre to the record-setting Burj Dubai, this iconic stretch of Sheikh Zayed Road defines the city's progress.**

This buzzing strip is known for the striking architecture of its high-rise residential buildings, office towers and top-class hotels. From the Dubai World Trade Centre to Interchange One (known as Defence Roundabout) the wide, skyscraping stretch of Sheikh Zayed Road – all 3.5km of it – is the subject of many a photo, as well as after-hours hook ups in the various happening hotspots. With so many residents, tourists and business people around, this area really buzzes at night, as the crowds flit from restaurants to bars to clubs.
*For **restaurants and bars** in the area, see p.226. For **shopping** see The Boulevard (p.156).*

## Downtown Burj Dubai

Sheikh Zayed Road, Interchange 1          www.burjdubai.com

Although it isn't expected to be completed until early 2009, the Burj Dubai became the tallest free-standing structure in the world on September 12 2007. The area surrounding the massive tower contains several community developments, Souk Al Bahar (p.165), the unfinished Dubai Mall, and two five-star hotels. The Palace hotel (p.49) has Asado steakhouse (p.227) while at Al Manzil you'll find Nezesaussi (p.232), an upmarket sports bar.  Map 4 D4 **31**

## Dubai World Trade Centre

04 332 1000

Trade Centre 2

www.dwtc.com

Flanked by impressive skyscrapers, Sheikh Zayed Road's
business district starts at the Dubai World Trade Centre and
exhibition halls (illustrated on the Dhs.100 banknote). When it
was completed in the 1970s, this 39 storey tower was the city's
tallest building. For a great view, try the Dhs.10 tour to the
observation deck (09:30 and 16:30 every day except Fridays;
leaving from the lobby information desk). Map 7 F2 **32**

## Emirates Towers

04 330 0000

Trade Centre 2

www.jumeirah.com

These twin towers are a true Dubai landmark. At 355m the
office tower was the tallest building in the Middle East and
Europe until the Burj Dubai surpassed it. The smaller tower, at
305m, houses the Emirates Towers hotel plus many eating and
drinking spots. The views from aptly named 51st floor Vu's Bar
(p.233), are superb. The Boulevard (p 156) is probably Dubai's
most exclusive mall. Map 7 D3 **33**

## Zabeel Park

Near Trade Centre Roundabout

Providing an oasis of greenery in the heart of downtown
Dubai, Zabeel Park has a technology theme and covers
51 hectares. There are recreational areas, a jogging track,
a mini cricket pitch, a football field, boating lake and an
amphitheatre. There are a number of restaurants and cafes for
a bite to eat too. Mondays are ladies only. Entry costs Dhs.5
for anyone over 2 years old. Map 5 A3 **34**

# If you only do one thing on...
# Sheikh Zayed Road

Put your finest clothes on and reserve a window seat at Vu's Bar (p.233), where the drinks are almost as good as the vistas.

## Best for...

**Sightseeing:** Get a bird's eye view of downtown from the observation deck at the top of Dubai's first skyscraper, the Dubai World Trade Centre (p.93).

**Shopping:** Treat yourself at The Boulevard at Emirates Towers (p.156), packed with Dubai's most exclusive designer boutiques.

**Relaxation:** Seek some high-rise pampering at the Fairmont's Willow Stream spa (p.139).

**Eating:** Fill up on some of the city's best steak at the Argentinean steakhouse, Asado (p.227).

**Drinking:** Get rowdy while enjoying daily drink deals at Scarlett's (p.233) in Emirates Towers.

Clockwise from to:: The Palace, Emirates Towers, Souk Al Bahar

# Umm Suqeim

With a world-famous hotel, sandy shores, art galleries, indoor ski slope and top shopping, this area is a must for any itinerary.

Nestled between Al Sufouh and Jumeira, Umm Suqeim is a pleasant family neighbourhood with a good stretch of beach and some excellent leisure and entertainment facilities. It is also home to Dubai's iconic landmark, the Burj Al Arab (p.47), which sits 280m off the coast on its own island.

Although not nearly as tall, the area's other luxury hotels are no less impressive, with fine-dining restaurants and some real star bars. Souk Madinat Jumeirah (p.98) should be on every visitor's to-do list for shopping and dining, while Wild Wadi Water Park (p.99) is a great place to cool down on a hot day. *For **restaurants and bars** in the area, see p.234. For **shopping,** see Souk Madinat Jumeirah (p.165) and Mall of the Emirates (p.162).*

## B21

04 340 3965

Behind Times Square, Al Quoz          www.b21gallery.com

This progressive art gallery represents around 20 Middle Eastern artists and is partnered with galleries in Europe. The result is a destination where collectors can source artwork and get advice on everything from finance to framing. Even if you're not in the market to buy, B21 hosts exhibitions by its steadily growing roster of talent. Map 3 E3 **35**

## Burj Al Arab

04 301 7777
Beach Road                                                              www.burj-al-arab.com

The Burj Al Arab is one of the most photographed sights in Dubai. The billowing-sail structure is a stunning piece of architecture – and inside it's no less spectacular. If your budget allows, you shouldn't miss the opportunity to sample luxury at the spa, bars and restaurants. Particularly recommended is afternoon tea at Sahn Eddar (p.237) or fine seafood dining at Al Mahara (p.236). Reservations are needed in advance. Map 3 C1 **36**

## The Jam Jar

04 341 7303
Behind Dubai Garden Centre, Al Quoz   www.jamjardubai.com

The Jam Jar is injecting a little culture to Sheikh Zayed Road. This small, bright gallery also offers wannabe Picassos the chance to paint their own works of art for a fixed price that includes unlimited paint, brushes and soft drinks. Prices start at Dhs.195 and rise to Dhs.230, depending on canvas size. Open 10:00 to 21:00 Monday to Thursday, 14:00 to 21:00 on Friday and closed Sunday. Map 3 D3 **37**

## Ski Dubai

04 409 4000
Mall of the Emirates                                                    www.skidxb.com

When you first see it, you might think Ski Dubai is some elaborate joke, such is its incongruous location in the middle of the mall. But the Middle East's first indoor ski slope is complete with black run, half-pipe, chair lifts and annoyingly cool instructors. Even if you don't ski, just looking at the slope is a spectacle not to be missed. The best views are from the restaurants and bars in the back of the mall, especially Après (p.240). A two-hour slope pass including equipment hire costs Dhs.220 – bring your own gloves.  Map 3 B3 **36**

### Souk Madinat Jumeirah
04 366 8888

Beach Road                                      www.madinatjumeirah.com

Souk Madinat Jumeirah (see shopping p.165) is located just a stone's throw from the Burj Al Arab. Built to resemble a traditional Arabian market, the souk is a maze of alleyways featuring 75 open-fronted shops and boutiques where you can find everything from swimwear to souvenirs. For weary shoppers, there are numerous coffee shops and bars, as well as Talise (p.138), an outstanding spa. This is also a popular destination for dining, including Moroccan food at Shoo Fee Ma Fee (p.238), and Chinese fusion at Zheng He (p.239).  Map 3 B1 **37**

### The Third Line
04 341 1367

Behind Times Square, Al Quoz              www.thethirdline.com

One of the leading lights of the Dubai art scene, The Third Line gallery in Al Quoz hosts exhibitions by artists originating from or working in the Middle East. There are indoor and outdoor spaces for shows, many of which have caught the eye of both local and international collectors. Open Saturday to Thursday 11:00 to 20:00.  Map 3 B1 **38**

### Umm Suqeim Beach

North of Jumeirah Beach Hotel

This lovely stretch of sand is on the Big Bus Tour (p.110) route and is one of the busiest public beaches at the weekends, especially Fridays. Visit mid-week to enjoy the golden sands and relatively clear waters. The jetty on the right provides a good spot for snorkelling but be aware of the currents. New lifeguard centres are being constructed at intervals along the beach, and while there are no toilet facilities at present there are several petrol stations nearby if nature calls. Map 3 D1 **39**

## Umm Suqeim Park

04 348 4554
parks@dm.gov.ae

Near Jumeirah Beach Hotel

This ladies' park is closed to men, except for at weekends. It is fairly large and has three big playgrounds with some great equipment that kids will love. There are also plenty of shady, grassy areas so that mums can sit and rest while the kids let off steam. In the middle of the park there is a popular coffee shop. Entrance is free. Map 3 D1 **40**

## Wild Wadi Water Park

04 348 4444
www.wildwadi.com

Near Jumeirah Beach Hotel

Spread over 12 acres beside Jumeirah Beach Hotel, this water park has 23 aquatic rides and attractions to suit all ages and bravery levels. Depending on how busy it is you may have to queue for some of the rides, but the wait is worth it. After paying the entrance fee there is no limit to the number of times you can ride. The park opens at 11:00 and the closing time depends on the time of year. Admission is Dhs.150 for adults and Dhs.125 for children. There is also a 'sundowner' rate (for the last three hours of opening), when adults pay Dhs.120 and children Dhs.95. Map 3 C1 **41**

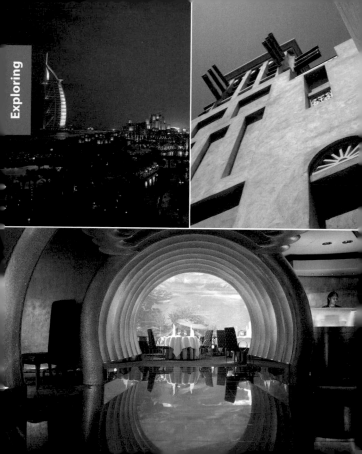

# If you only do one thing in...
# Umm Suqeim

After browsing Souk Madinat Jumeirah head to the beach and watch the sun set behind the Burj Al Arab.

## Best for...

**Relaxation:** Rent out a private bungalow in the well-manicured grounds of the Talise spa (p.139) at the Souk Madinat Jumeirah.

**Drinking:** Down a cocktail at Après (p.240) after you down Ski Dubai's slopes.

**Sightseeing:** The views of the Burj Al Arab are extraordinary from Wild Wadi's Jumeirah Sceirah (p.99).

**Eating:** Shoo Fee Ma Fee (p.238) at Madinat Jumeirah serves up some of the city's finest Moroccan cuisine.

**Shopping:** Explore the alleyways of Souk Madinat Jumeirah (p.165) and discover the perfect gift to take back home.

Clockwise from top: Madinat Jumeirah and the Burj Al Arab, a windtower, Al Mahara

# Further Out

**The United Arab Emirates offers visitors some spectacular sights, from ancient forts to mountain pools and seemingly infinite deserts.**

Venture from the hotel pool and air-conditioned malls, hire a car and start exploring the area. This part of the world has a lot more to offer than the obvious city sights and many are just a short drive away. Close to Dubai, nature lovers should check out Ras Al Khor Wildlife Sanctuary (Ras Al Khor Road, 04 206 4240), the only nature reserve within the city and a great place for bird watchers, with 1,500 flamingos. If you prefer pounding hooves to flapping wings then head to Dubai Racing Club (04 336 3666; www.nadalshebaclub.com) for horse racing.

Quite simply, heading out of Dubai to the other cities and emirates can be hugely rewarding and will add a unique cultural perspective to your time in the UAE.

## Sharjah

Before Dubai's rise to prominence as a trading and tourism hotspot, neighbouring Sharjah was one of the wealthiest towns in the region, with settlers earning their livelihood from fishing, pearling and trade. Sharjah is worth a visit for its various museums and great shopping. Its commitment to art, culture and preserving its traditional heritage is well known throughout the Arab world. Sharjah is built around Khalid

Lagoon (popularly known as the creek), and the surrounding Buheirah Corniche is a popular spot for an evening stroll. From various points on the lagoon, small dhows can be hired to see the lights of the city from the water.

The Heritage Area (06 569 3999; www.sharjahtourism.ae), is a fascinating old walled city, home to numerous museums and the traditional Souk Al Arsah. The nearby Arts Area is a treat for art lovers with galleries and more museums. Another must is Al Qasba (06 556 0777; www.qaq.ae), Sharjah's latest attraction which has performance spaces and waterside restaurants. Another worthy stop-off is the Sharjah Natural History Museum (06 531 1411; www.sharjahtourism.ae).

Shoppers shouldn't miss the beautiful Central Souk, also known as the Blue Souk. The two buildings contain more than 600 shops selling gold, and knick-knacks. This is one of the best places in the UAE to buy carpets.

## Abu Dhabi

Dubai is often mistaken as the capital of the UAE – but that honour belongs to Abu Dhabi. Oil was discovered there before Dubai (1958 compared with 1966) and today it accounts for 10% of the world's known crude oil reserves. It is therefore no surprise that Abu Dhabi is the richest emirate in the UAE. In recent years, there has been a greater commitment to tourism, and new developments are sprouting up all over the emirate. It is home to numerous internationally renowned hotels, a selection of shiny shopping malls and a sprinkling of culture in the form of heritage sites and souks. The malls are much less busy than in Dubai, and goods are sometimes cheaper.

Travellers to the city shouldn't miss the Sheikh Zayed Grand Mosque between the Mussafah and Maqta bridges. The recently finished mosque covers 22,000sqm and is the sixth-largest mosque in the world. During the cooler months, the blue tile-covered corniche on the gulf-side of the city is a great place for an evening stroll.

Outside the city, Abu Dhabi emirate is home to the oasis towns of Al Ain and Liwa. The Al Ain Museum (03 764 1595; www.aam.gov.ae) illustrates various aspects of life in the UAE and includes a selection of photographs, Bedouin jewellery and archeological displays. It is also worth taking a trip to the Liwa oasis where the spectacular dunes are a photographer's dream. Liwa lies at the edge of the Rub Al Khali (Empty Quarter), one of the largest sand deserts in the world.

# Northern Emirates

North of Dubai and Sharjah are Ajman, Umm Al Quwain and Ras Al Khaimah. These three emirates are much smaller in size than Dubai and Abu Dhabi and are also less developed.

Ajman is the smallest of the emirates, but its proximity to Dubai and Sharjah has enabled it to grow considerably. It has one of the largest dhow building centres in the region, offering a chance to see these massive wooden boats being built with rudimentary tools, using skills passed down through the generations. Ajman also has some great beaches and a pleasant corniche. Much of the nightlife revolves around the Ajman Kempinski Hotel & Resort (06 714 5555; www.ajmankempinski.com) with its dining and entertainment options.

Umm Al Quwain has the smallest population and little has changed over the years. It is home to Dreamland Aqua Park (www.dreamlanduae.com), the largest waterpark in the Middle East with over 25 rides. Two of the most interesting activities Umm Al Quwain has to offer are crab hunting (p.122) and mangrove tours. The Flamingo Beach Resort (06 765 0000; www.flamingoresort.ae) offers both tours.

Ras Al Khaimah is the most northerly of the seven emirates, but thanks to the new Emirates Road extension you can make the trip from Dubai in less than an hour. With the jagged Hajar Mountains rising just behind the city, and the Arabian Gulf stretching out from the shore, RAK has some of the best scenery in the UAE. A creek divides the city into the old town and the newer Al Nakheel district. For a day trip, you should go the souk in the old town and the National Museum of Ras Al Khaimah (07 233 3411; www.rakmuseum.gov.ae). This is a good starting point for exploring the surrounding countryside and visiting the ancient sites of Ghalilah and Shimal.

## Hatta

The road leading to Hatta from Dubai (E44) is a trip in itself. Watch as the sand gradually changes from beige to dark orange and then disappears, only to be replaced by jagged mountains. The famous Big Red sand dune lies on this road, and is a popular spot for dune driving in 4WDs or quad bikes.

Hatta is a small town, nestled at the food of the Hajar Mountains, about 100km from Dubai city and 10km the Dubai-Oman border. It is home to the oldest fort in the Dubai emirate, which was built in 1790. You'll also see several watchtowers on the surrounding hills. On the drive you'll pass a row of carpet shops, ideal for putting your bargaining skills into practice. The town itself has a sleepy, relaxed feel, and includes the Heritage Village (04 852 1374), which charts the area's 3,000 history and includesa 200 year-old mosque and the fortress built by Sheikh Maktoum bin Hasher Al Maktoum in 1896, which is now used as a weaponry museum

Beyond the village and into the mountains are the Hatta Pools, where you can see deep, strangely shaped canyons carved out by rushing floodwater. For tours see p.111.

The trail towards the pools is graded, so a two wheel drive car and some skilled driving should be enough to get you there. To get to the pools from the Dubai-Hatta road, take a right at the fort roundabout, then left towards the Heritage Village, another left at the roundabout, and then the first main right. After driving through a second village, the tarmac will end and you will see a gravel track on your right. The Hatta Fort Hotel (04 852 3211; www.jebelali-international. com) offers bungalow-style luxury rooms and plenty of sports and leisure facilities including shooting and mini-golf.

## East Coast

Even if you're only in the UAE for a short time, a trip to the East Coast is a must. You can get there in less than two hours.

The diving is considered better than that off Dubai's coast, mainly because of increased visibility. Snoopy Island on Dibba's coast is a favourite spot for snorkelling. The East Coast is home to a few interesting spots, many of which are free to explore. The site of the oldest mosque in the UAE,

Badiyah, is roughly half way down the East Coast, north of Khor Fakkan. The building is believed to date back to the middle of the 15th century and was restored in 2003. The village is considered one of the oldest settlements on the East Coast, which is thought to have been inhabited since 3000BC. Located at the northernmost point of the East Coast, Dibba is made up of three fishing villages, each coming under a different jurisdiction: Sharjah, Fujairah, and Oman. The villages share an attractive bay and excellent diving locations. The Hajar Mountains provide a wonderful backdrop to the public beaches. Further north across the border into Oman is Khasab, a great base for exploring the inlets and unspoilt waters of Musandam. You can stay at the Golden Tulip (968 26 73 07 77; www.goldentulipkhasab.com), who can organise dhow cruises and dolphin watching, both of which are recommended.

Further south on the coast lies Fujairah, the youngest of the seven emirates. Overlooking the atmospheric old town is a fort, that is reportedly about 300 years old. The surrounding hillsides are dotted with more such ancient forts and watchtowers, which add an air of mystery and charm. Dubai residents often use Fujairah as a base for exploring the rest of the coast. Hotels include Le Meridien Al Aqah (09 244 9000; www.starwoodhotels.com), and JAL Fujairah Hotel & Spa (09 244 9700; www.jalhotels.com).

Khor Kalba sits just south of Fujairah and is the most northerly mangrove forest in the world, and home to a variety of plant, marine and birdlife not found anywhere else in the UAE. A canoe tour by Desert Rangers (p.113) is the best way to reach the heart of the mangrove reserve.

# Tours & Sightseeing

**Whether it be by plane, boat or 4WD, taking a tour is one of the most fun and efficient ways to see a different side to the emirates.**

Navigating the city by taxi can be pretty easy, but exploring the surrounding areas often proves a bit more difficult without the help of a guide. Boat tours are a great way to see the city from afar while enjoying the clear gulf water. Helicopter and plane tours give the most extensive look at the growing city, while bus tours offer plenty of information and more user-friendly schedules. No visitor should leave without experiencing a driving safari of some sort. Many of the operators listed offer a wide range of tours and activities so it's worth ringing around to see which suit your budget and timescale.

## Boat & Yacht Charters

### Bluesail Dubai

04 397 9730

Near British Embassy, Bur Dubai     www.bluesailyachts.com

Bluesail has two 42ft yachts available for private charter. It also offers private motorboat charters on its new 21ft/200hp and 34ft/450hp speedboats, taking in the creek and blasting out into the Gulf along Dubai's coastline. The skipper will evevn give you the wheel following a safety and tactics briefing. All vessels are fully insured and fitted with the required safety equipment.  Map 5 C3 **42**

Musandam

### Bristol Middle East Yacht Solution    04 366 3538
Marina Walk, Dubai Marina    sylvie@bristol-middleeast.com

This marina-based company offers charters and packages
on boats of all kind, from luxury yachts to Captain Jack, its
old wooden dhow. Its boats can be hired for events, from
romantic outings for two to weddings and birthday parties.
Fishing trips and watersports can be organised too, and
Bristol can also put together land and air tours.   Map 2 D2 43

### Tour Dubai    04 336 8409
Various Locations    www.tour-dubai.com

Tour Dubai offers a one-hour creek tour aboard a traditional
dhow, including pre-recorded commentary covering the
UAE's history and places of interest (available in English).

There are four departures a day (11:30, 13:30, 15:30 and 17:30), and the price of around Dhs.70 includes transfers to and from your hotel. The company offers a variety of other tours, including private dhow charters.

## Bus Tours

### The Big Bus Company
04 324 4187
Wafi City, Oud Metha
www.bigbus.co.uk

The open-air London double-decker buses roaming the streets of Dubai belong to The Big Bus Company. There's live commentary in English, which includes little-known trivia such as the fact that in 1968 there were only 13 cars in Dubai. It's wise to break the tour at the recommended stops and then hop on the following bus once you've finished exploring. Prices are Dhs.150 for adults; children are Dhs.100 (ages 5 to 15 years); free for children under 5 years; families pay Dhs.400 (two adults and two children). Tours run daily with departures every hour from 09:00 to 17:00.

### Wonder Bus Tours
04 359 5656
BurJuman, Bur Dubai
www.wonderbusdubai.com

The Wonder Bus is an amphibious vehicle capable of doing 120kph on the road and seven knots on water (life jackets are supplied). The two-hour trips concentrate on the creek. The bus is air conditioned and can take 44 passengers. Prices are Dhs.115 for adults; children cost Dhs.75 (ages 3 to 12). There are three departures daily: 11:30, 14:30 and 17:00 but this is subject to change depending on tides.

# Desert & Mountain Safaris

Many of the main tour operators listed on page 113 offer similar tours and packages. Below are explanations for some of the most popular options. Once you've decided on the one for you, call the companies for price comparisons.

## Desert Safari

Enjoy some thrilling desert driving before settling down to watch the sun set. Starting around 16:00, the tour passes fascinating scenery that provides great photo opportunities. You then enjoy a delicious dinner and the calm of a starlit night at an Arabian campsite before returning around 22:00.

## Full-Day Safari

These tours usually pass traditional Bedouin villages and camel farms in the desert, with a drive through sand dunes of varying colours and heights. Most tours also visit Fossil Rock and the mesmerising Hajar Mountains, the highest in the UAE. A cold buffet lunch may be provided in the mountains before the drive home.

## Hatta Pools Safari

Hatta (p.105) is a quiet, old-fashioned town famed for its freshwater rock pools. The full-day trip usually includes a stop at the Hatta Fort Hotel, where you can enjoy the pool, landscaped gardens, archery, clay pigeon shooting and nine-hole golf course. Lunch is served either in the hotel, or in the mountains. The trip costs from Dhs.260 to Dhs.345.

### Mountain Safari
This full-day tour takes you north along the coast, heading inland and entering the Hajar Mountains at Wadi Bih. You travel through rugged canyons onto steep tracks, past mountainsides and stone houses. It leads to Dibba where a highway takes you to Dubai, stopping at Masafi Market on the way.

### Overnight Safari
This 24 hour tour starts at about 15:00 with a drive through the dunes to a Bedouin-style campsite. Dine under the stars, sleep in the fresh air and wake to the smell of freshly brewed coffee, before heading for the mountains. The drive takes you through rugged scenery, past dunes and along wadis, before stopping for a buffet lunch and returning to Dubai.

## Helicopter & Seaplane Charters

### Aerogulf Services Company          04 220 0331
Dubai International Airport          www.aerogulfservices.com
Viewing Dubai from the air is an exhilarating way to get a unique perspective of the city. These tours will show you parks, the creek, palaces and beaches. The tours operate during daylight hours. Rates are Dhs.2,925 for a half-hour tour (basic) and Dhs.3,600 for a 'VIP class' half-hour tour.

### Seawings          04 883 2999
Jebel Ali Golf Resort & Spa, Jebel Ali          www.seawings.ae
See Dubai from an eight-seater Cessna 208 Caravan seaplane. This experience gives you a breathtaking view of the city's

attractions, soaring past and over Dubai Marina, the Jumeira and Jebel Ali Palms, the World and downtown Dubai, before touching down smoothly again on the water at Jebel Ali. Prices start at Dhs.795 for a seat on the half-hour flight, or you can opt for an upgrade with the extended, more luxurious 'gold tour'.

# Hot Air Ballooning

### Balloon Adventures Dubai
04 273 8585
Near Claridge Hotel, Deira      www.ballooning.ae

Operating two of the most advanced and largest hot air balloons in the world, with a capacity of up to 40 people, Balloon Adventures offer tours for individuals and groups. Flights begin around 05:00 between October and May in order to catch the sunrise, and afterwards you can go off-road driving over the dunes with experienced drivers as part of the trip.

### Desert Rangers
04 340 2408
Dubai Garden Centre, Al Quoz      www.desertrangers.com

Desert Rangers operates balloon trips so you can sample absolute silence as you float over the desert at either dusk or dawn. You finish this memorable experience with refreshments on landing. It is advisable to book these popular trips early. Flights are subject to weather conditions on the day. Pick up for the morning balloon safari is 04:30. Trips operate from October to May (with some September flights) and the cost is Dhs.750 per person.

# Main Tour Operators

### Absolute Adventure

04 345 9900

Near Golden Tulip Hotel, Dibba          www.adventure.ae

Absolute Adventure offers dormitory-style camping (food and washing facilities are included) in a traditional stone bungalow on the East Coast. Choose from a range of adrenaline-pumped activities such as treks exploring ancient ruins, sea kayaking, snorkelling, mountain biking and motor hang-gliding. Activity prices start at Dhs.200.

### Arabian Adventures

04 303 4888

Emirates Holiday Bld, Bur Dubai  www.arabian-adventures.com

Offering a range of tours and activities, Arabian Adventures tailors tours to meet individual needs. It organises itineraries for complete trips and can provide specific services. The tours available include sand skiing or boarding, moonlight dhow cruises, city tours, desert safaris, camel riding and wadi and dune bashing. Car rental is also available.

### Desert Rangers

04 340 2408

Dubai Garden Centre, Al Quoz          www.desertrangers.com

In addition to the standard range of desert and mountain safaris, Desert Rangers offers several other exciting activities and tours. The scope of its activities is wide-ranging and covers camel trekking by day or night, sand boarding, canoeing, raft building, deep sea fishing, dhow cruises, camping, hiking, rock climbing, Hatta Pool safaris, desert driving courses, dune buggying and helicopter tours of Dubai.

## Dubai Tourist & Travel Services     04 336 7727

Al Abbar Building, Bur Dubai     www.dubai-travel.ae

DTTS offers Dubai, Abu Dhabi and Al Ain city and shopping tours, creek dinner cruises, Sharjah-Ajman cultural tours, East Coast tours, desert and mountain tours to Hatta, sand skiing, camel riding, desert safaris and overnight trips.

## Gulf Ventures     04 209 5568

Near Gold Souk, Deira     www.gulfventures.ae

Gulf Ventures is local company with good knowledge of culture, history and the lay of the land in Dubai. It offers a variety of exciting and informative tours over a wide area of the UAE and Oman, including Bedouin camps, creek cruises, tours around other cities and the East Coast, plus activities such as fishing, polo and ballooning, in addition to a number of city tours.

## Net Tours     050 659 5506

Le Meridien Mina Seyahi, Al Sufouh     www.nettoursdubai.com

Net Tours covers most of what Dubai can bestow in terms of adventure; everything from mountain tours to theme parks and dhow cruises to safaris. Delve into Dubai's history, trek through Ras Al Khaimah's mountains or try sand skiing in a range of tours. Five desert campsites 45 minutes from Dubai allow you to explore the dunes and return to your Bedouin haven in an 'authentic' Arabian adventure that comes complete with air-conditioning, separate bathroom facilities for men and women, internet, satellite connection and even a VIP lounge.

Tours & Sightseeing

### Oasis Palm Tourism
04 262 8889

Al Rigga Road, opposite ADCB, Deira · www.opdubai.com

Oasis Palm's desert safaris, dhow dinner cruises and wadi trips come with the typical guarantee of the desired Arabian adventure, alongside the promise of great service and a memorable experience. Its East Coast tours will take you through the Hajar Mountains and the strawberry garden in Al Dhaid to one of the oldest mosques in the UAE. It also offer diving trips to the beautiful Khor Fakkan (the 'creek of two jaws') and four-hour deep sea fishing trips.

### Off-Road Adventures
04 405 2917

Shangri-La, Trade Centre 1 · www.arabiantours.com

As its name suggests, this company offers a wide range of off-road excursions, including desert trips (including dinner at an Arabian camp), wadi and mountain drives, overnight camping trips, and expeditions to Liwa and the Empty Quarter. In addition to off-road tours, it also arranges watersports and airborne activities, and can offer tailor-made packages for groups.

### Orient Tours
04 282 8238

Various Locations · www.orienttours.ae

Orient Tours offers trips to all major cities in the UAE, including trips to the horse and camel races, desert safaris, sea safaris around Musandam, off-road trips to Hatta and day tours of the majestic dunes of the Empty Quarter in Liwa. It offers flexible packages catering to individual needs.

Close-up camel

## Voyagers Xtreme

Dune Centre, Satwa

04 345 4504
www.turnertraveldubai.com

Voyagers Xtreme provides a range of adventurous activities over land, sea and air. For a trip to remember, try its adventurous 'One Wild Week in the Emirates' tour. You will visit places such as the Empty Quarter, Al Ain, the Hajar Mountains, Fossil Rock, the East Coast, Dibba, Musandam and Wadi Bih, and enjoy activities as diverse as mountain biking, trekking, desert driving, hot air ballooning, snorkelling and sky diving.

# Sports & Spas

# Active Dubai

**Dubai has a wealth of spas, sports and resorts dedicated to the art of relaxation.**

It is not just the shops and beaches that are attracting visitors to the emirates. In an effort to appeal to all travellers, Dubai is investing heavily in professional and recreational sports and luxurious sporting facilities. The Dubai World Cup is the richest horse race in the world, the Dubai Rugby 7s regularly pulls in crowds in excess of 70,000 and the Dubai Tennis Championships see the world's leading players compete in an intimate setting.

In an effort to appeal to keen golfers, several fine courses have been built, many designed by leading lights such as Robert Trent Jones II and Nick Faldo. More are set to open in the near future, including one designed by Tiger Woods in Dubailand (p.265).

Dubai's range of activities doesn't end there. Traditional sports, such as camel racing and falconry, have been encouraged by the government as a means of preserving national heritage. The city's location between the Arabian Gulf and desert allows for an interesting mix of watersports such as diving and crab hunting, and unique sand-based activities including dune-driving and sand skiing.

Best of all, Dubai's spa culture caters to both athletes and loungers, and the wide range of treatments available means you could sample something new every day of your stay.

Clockwise from top left: Climbing Fossil Rock, underwater life, golf in New Dubai

Sports & Activities

Take advantage of Dubai's clear waters, unique heritage and miles of dunes. Hop on a camel, dhow or jetski, pick up your clubs or just swim with the fish.

## Camel Rides

When in Arabia, meeting a camel is a must. You could opt for a short camel ride as part of a desert tour (p.111) or a hotel package, but for a more memorable experience you should go on a longer guided jaunt in the sand dunes. On these tours there are stops for rests, refreshments and photos, so that you can remember your experience long after the aches subside.

### Al Ain Golden Sands Camel Safaris    03 768 8006
Hilton Al Ain, Al Ain

This company offers a selection of tours that include a camel ride over the dunes of Bida Bint Saud. The rides usually last between one and two and a half hours. Transfers to Al Ain, Arabic coffee, dates and soft drinks are included.

## Crab Hunting

### Lama Desert Tours    04 334 4330
Near Lamcy Plaza, Karama    www.lamadubai.com

This unusual tour takes you to Umm Al Quwain where you head out to sea to hunt crabs, and then dine on your own clawed catch of the day. The cost is Dhs.280 per person

Early morning at the camel track

(minimum six people) and includes return transfers, soft drinks, snacks and a crab dinner. Not recommended if you don't like seafood.

## Dhow Charters

### Al Boom Tourist Village
04 324 3000

Near Garhoud Bridge, Oud Metha
www.alboom.ae

Al Boom Tourist Village operates nine dhows on the creek, ranging from single-deckers with room for 20 people, right up to the huge triple-decker Mumtaz, which can take 350 passengers. It offers a variety of packages, with prices varying accordingly. As well as the usual dinner cruises, late-night trips can also be arranged. Map 5 C4 **3**

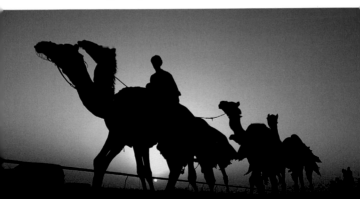

### Khasab Travel & Tours
04 266 9950

Warba Centre, Deira
www.khasabtours.com

Sailing north from Dibba this cruise follows the coastline where steep rocky cliffs rise out of the sea. You'll pass small fishing villages that are accessible only by boat, and will hopefully see dolphins and turtles. Prices start at Dhs.200 per adult for a full day, including lunch and refreshments.

## Golf

The number of international-standard courses grows each year, with recent additions including the Four Seasons within Dubai Festival City (p.159). The world's first course designed by Tiger Woods will be created in Dubailand and is set to open in late 2009. Ernie Els's eponymous club will be in the same development.

Dubai Golf operates a central reservation system for those wishing to book a round on any of the major courses in the emirate. For further information visit www.dubaigolf.com or email booking@dubaigolf.com.

### Arabian Ranches Golf Club
04 366 3000

Arabian Ranches
www.arabianranchesgolfdubai.com

Designed by Ian Baker-Finch in association with Nicklaus Design, this par 72 grass course uses the natural desert terrain and features indigenous shrubs and bushes. You must have an official handicap to play, but can reserve a tee-off time six days in advance. Facilities include a golf academy with floodlit driving range, an extensive short game practice area, and GPS on all golf carts.

## Dubai Creek Golf & Yacht Club
04 295 6000

Opposite Deira City Centre, Deira    www.dubaigolf.com

Dubai Creek Golf & Yacht Club has recently undergone a major redevelopment, with a challenging new front nine redesigned by Thomas Bjorn. The par 71 championship course is open to all players holding a valid handicap certificate. Those who are new to the game are encouraged to join the golf academy manned by PGA-qualified instructors. There is also a new nine-hole par three course, a floodlit driving range and extensive short game practice facilities. Map 5 C4 **6**

## Emirates Golf Club
04 380 2222

Interchange Five, Sheikh Zayed Road    www.dubaigolf.com

Emirates Golf Club has two 18 hole championship courses to choose from. The par 71 Majlis Course was the first grass course in the Middle East and plays host to the annual Dubai Desert Classic (p.131). The Wadi Course reopened in October 2006 following a major redesign. The club also offers the Peter Cowen Golf Academy, along with two driving ranges and dedicated practice areas. Map 2 E2 **7**

## Four Seasons Golf Club
04 601 0101

Dubai Festival City, Garhoud    www.fourseasons.com

World-renowned golf course designer Robert Trent Jones II is behind the Four Seasons offering. Lying at the heart of Dubai Festival City, beside the creek, the resort enjoys great views across the city. The 7,250 yard par 72 Championship Course has a plush clubhouse and extensive water features.
Map 6 C3 **8**

### Montgomerie Golf Club          04 390 5600
The Montgomerie, Emirates Hills   www.themontgomerie.com

Set on 200 acres of land, The Montgomerie was designed by
Colin Montgomerie and Desmond Muirhead. The 18 hole,
par 72 course has some unique characteristics, including the
mammoth 656 yard 18th hole. Golfing facilities include a
driving range, putting greens, a floodlit par three course and
a swing analysis studio, while the newly opened clubhouse
boasts guest rooms, a spa, and various bars and restaurants,
including Nineteen (p.200).   Map 2 D3 **9**

### The Resort Course          · 04 883 6000
Jebel Ali Hotel, Jebel Ali        www.jebelali-international.com

Situated in the landscaped gardens of the Jebel Ali Golf
Resort & Spa, this nine-hole, par 36 course offers golfers fine
views of the Arabian Gulf. Renowned for its good condition
all year round, the Resort Course is also home to the Jebel Ali
Golf Resort & Spa Challenge, the curtain raiser to the Dubai
Desert Classic (p.130).

## Hot Air Ballooning & Parasailing

A magical way of seeing the the sun rise over the sand dunes
is by hot air balloon. Balloon Adventures Dubai and Desert
Rangers (p.113) both offer these memorable trips.

If you'd like an an aerial view of the Palm Jumeirah but
can't afford a helicopter then pop down to the beach for a
spot of parasailing. The area around the marina is the place
to be; the Sheraton Jumeirah Beach (04 399 5533) has a
watersports and activity centre, and Nautica 1992 (050 426

2415) operates from the Habtoor Grand. Summertime Marine Sports (04 329 5211) also offers flights from the open beach near Le Meridien Mina Seyahi hotel (04 399 3333). All use specially designed boats with winches and a launch pad on the back, meaning you no longer have to sprint down the beach (or get dragged through the sand) in order to get airborne. You can expect to pay around Dhs.250 for a 15 to 20 minute ride, or Dhs.350 for the tandem option.

## Wadi & Dune Bashing

Most car rental agencies offer visitors 4WDs capable of desert driving (p.43). If renting a 4WD, make sure you get the details of the insurance plan. Most rental insurers won't cover damage caused by off-roading. Dune bashing, or desert driving, is one of the toughest challenges for both car and driver, but once you have mastered this skill, it's also the most fun. If you want a wilderness adventure but don't know where to start, contact any of the major tour companies (p.113). All offer a range of desert and mountain safaris.

Driving in wadis is usually a bit more straightforward. Wadis are (usually) dry gullies, carved through the rock by rushing floodwaters, following the course of seasonal rivers. The main safety precaution to take when wadi bashing is to keep your eyes open for rare, but not impossible, thunder storms developing. The wadis can fill up quickly and you will need to make your way to higher ground pretty fast to avoid flash floods.

For further information and tips on driving off-road in the emirates check out the *UAE Off-Road Explorer*.

# Watersports & Diving

Most beachside hotels offer both guests and visitors a range of watersports, including sea kayaking, sailing and windsurfing. Some hotels require that non-guests pay beach fees in order to access the facilities, while others will let you enter the beach area for free if you make a reservation at the watersports desk beforehand. Contact the Habtoor Grand (04 399 5000) and Le Meridien Mina Seyahi (04 399 3333).

Diving is popular and the clear waters of the coast are home to a variety of marine species, coral life and even shipwrecks. You'll see some exotic fish and possibly moray eels, small sharks, barracuda, sea snakes and stingrays. Most of the wrecks are on the west coast, while the flora and fauna can be seen on the east coast. Another great option for diving enthusiasts is a trip to Musandam. Part of the Sultanate of Oman, it is often described as the 'Norway of the Middle East' due to its many inlets and the way the cliffs plunge directly into the sea.

Sheer wall dives with strong currents and clear waters are more suitable for advanced divers, while the huge bays with their calm waters and bountiful shallow reefs are ideal for the less experienced. A selection of the UAE's diving companies is listed below. Courses are offered under the usual international training organisations. More details on specific dives and sites can be found in the *UAE Underwater Explorer*.

### Al Boom Diving                    04 342 2993
Near Iranian Hospital, Satwa          www.alboomdiving.com

Al Boom is a purpose-built school with a fully outfitted diving shop. There is a variety of courses on offer, both here and at its PADI Gold Palm Resort at Le Meridien Al Aqah Beach Resort (09 204 4912) near Fujairah. Map 4 E1 **11**

### The Pavilion Dive Centre    04 406 8827
Jumeirah Beach Hotel    www.thepaviliondivecentre.com

This is run by PADI course directors, who offer an extensive range of courses for beginners through to instructors. Daily dive charters for certified divers are available in Dubai, and trips to Musandam can be organised upon request. Two dives with full equipment in Dubai are priced at Dhs.300, and two dives with full equipment in Musandam cost Dhs.490 including transport and lunch. Map 3 C1 **12**

### Scuba Dubai    04 341 4940
DWTC Apartments, Trade Centre 2    www.scubadubai.com

For those wishing to arrange their own diving and snorkelling trips, equipment can be rented from Scuba Dubai on a 24 hour basis. Rates for Thursday, Friday and Saturday are the same as renting for one day because the shop is closed on Fridays. Note that original diving certification must be shown for all equipment rentals. Map 7 F2 **13**

### Scubatec    04 334 8988
Sana Building, Karama

Scubatec is a five-star IDC licensed by PADI and TDI. Lessons are provided in Arabic, English, German or Urdu, and the company offers a full range of courses from beginner to instructor level. A variety of dive trips is available in Dubai and on the East Coast. Map 5 B2 **14**

# Spectator Sports

**Dubai has the best line-up of international sport in the region, with world-class tennis, golf and horse racing among the highlights.**

Dubai has been expanding its repertoire of sporting events on two fronts. The government has made efforts to promote traditional sports; the best example of this can be found at the Friday camel races held throughout the country, and in Dubai at Nad Al Sheba.

The emirate has also steadily been backing huge international events that not only capture the local imagination, but draw sporting enthusiasts from around the world. One big advantage of these is that crowds are smaller than in other countries and tickets are more freely available, although you'll have to be quick.

## Camel Racing

This is a chance to see a truly traditional local sport up close. Apart from great photo opportunities and the excitement of the races, you can also have a browse around the track-side market. This is where you'll see old traders hand-weaving camel halters and lead ropes.

Races take place at Nad Al Sheba (04 327 0077; www. dubairacingclub.com) during the winter months, usually on Thursday and Friday mornings. Races start very early (by about 07:30) and are usually over by 08:30. Admission is free.

Dubai Tennis Championships

# Golf

### Dubai Desert Classic
Emirates Golf Club

04 380 2222
www.dubaidesertclassic.com

One of the highlights of the Dubai sporting calendar, this European PGA Tour competition is a popular event among both players and spectators at the end of January and start of February. Tiger Woods won the 2006 and 2008 tournaments. Tickets for the event at Emirates Golf Club sell out fast, so check the website regularly for details.   Map 2 E2  **7**

# Horse Racing

### Dubai Racing Club
Nad Al Sheba Racecourse

04 332 2277
www.dubairacingclub.com

A visit to Dubai during the winter months is not complete without experiencing race night at Nad Al Sheba. Top

jockeys from Australia, Europe and the USA regularly compete throughout the season (October to April). The start time is 19:00 (except during Ramadan when it is 21:00). The clubhouse charges day membership on race nights. Everyone can take part in various free competitions to select the winning horses, with the ultimate aim of taking home prizes or cash. The dress code for the public enclosures is casual, while racegoers are encouraged to dress smart-casual in the clubhouse and private viewing boxes. General admission and parking are free and the public has access to most areas. Nad Al Sheba also plays host to the world's richest horse race, the Dubai World Cup, every March. You can also catch a slightly more raw form of horseracing at Jebel Ali racecourse, near The Greens, every other Friday afternoon during the season.

## Motorsports

The vast amount of desert and rugged terrain in the Emirates has long been a playground for off-road rallying. More recently, traditional motorsports have gained prominence, with the Gulf on its way to becoming well known on the Grand Prix circuit. Starting in 2009, Abu Dhabi will host a leg of the Formula One World Championship (www.abudhabigp.com).

Dubai Autodrome (www.dubaiautodrome.com) is an FIA-approved circuit, and hosts legs of international racing series. Off-road enthusiasts can still find excitement in the annual UAE Desert Challenge (p.39).

# Rugby

### Dubai Rugby Sevens
Al Ain Road

04 321 0008
www.dubairugby7s.com

One of the biggest events in the UAE, sport or non-sport related, the Dubai Rugby 7s attracted more than 70,000 people in 2007. The two-day event is the first stop in the IRB Sevens World series and plays host to the top 16 sevens teams in the world. The first day of the event sees regional teams go head to head while the second day lets the big boys take the pitch. Sevens often proves exciting for fans due to its fast pace and high scores. Tickets regularly sell out weeks in advance so make sure you plan early. Starting in 2008, the event will be held at a new rugby complex near Silicon Valley. The exact location has yet to be determined.

# Tennis

### Dubai Tennis Championships
Dubai Tennis Stadium

04 282 4122
www.dubaitennischampionships.com

The Dubai Tennis Championships take place every February at the Aviation Club in Garhoud, and offer a great opportunity to catch some of the top players in the game at close quarters. The $1 million event is firmly established on the international tennis calendar, and features both men's and ladies' tournaments. Andy Roddick took the men's title in 2008. Tickets for the later stages sell out in advance so keep an eye out for sale details, although entrance to some of the earlier rounds can be bought on the day. Map 6 C1 17

# Spas

**Take some time out from the city's frenetic pace to enjoy a massage, facial or hammam – you won't have to go far to find one.**

The city's focus on luxury tourism is a godsend for people who love to be pampered. Nearly every five-star hotel has at least one spa, many of which are renovated every few years to keep up with the latest developments and design trends. Several venues utilise brand name treatment products, while others focus on unique types of treatments, such as Moroccan baths.

Men-specific treatments and male-only spas are increasing in popularity. Keep in mind that the range of spas is huge, and many of the lesser known options are just as good and often cheaper. Jumeira has several smaller spas, treatment centres and nail salons such as The Haven (p.138) and Elche (p.136) that cater for those on a smaller budget.

## 1847

04 399 8989
Grosvenor House, Dubai Marina
info@1847.ae

Considered the first dedicated 'grooming lounge' for men in the Middle East, 1847 offers manicures, professional shaves and several styles of massage in a decidedly 'manly' setting. Several of the treatments take place in private 'studies,' complete with personal LCD TVs. In addition to the Grosvenor House branch, there is another 1847 lounge in The Boulevard at Emirates Towers (04 330 1847). Map 2 D2 **18**

Willow Stream Spa & Health Club

## Akaru Spa

04 282 8578
www.akaruspa.com

The Aviation Club, Garhoud

The autumnal colours, natural decor, wooden fittings and glass features create a truly tranquil retreat at this Garhoud favourite. Exotic treatments range from various specialised facials and wraps to microdermabrasion. During the cooler months Akaru offers treatments that are administered on the rooftop terrace. Map 6 C1 **17**

## Amara Spa

04 602 1660
www.dubai.park.hyatt.com

Park Hyatt Dubai, Deira

There is no communal changing room or wet area here, instead you are escorted directly to your treatment room, which acts as your personal spa. Here you have all the facilities of a changing room as well as a relaxation corner. After your treatment enjoy a shower under the sun in your very own private outdoor shower and relaxation area. This is one of the few places in Dubai to offer a massage space for couples. Map 9 C4 **19**

## Assawan Spa & Health Club

Burj Al Arab, Umm Suqeim

04 301 7480
www.burj-al-arab.com

The Assawan Spa is situated on the 18th floor of the breathtaking Burj Al Arab. Unsurprisingly, it's an elaborate spot with a mosaic-covered ceiling and ornately tiled corridors. The personal service is excellent. The spa has female-only and mixed environments, including a state-of-the-art gym with studios (where you can take part in everything from yoga to aerobics), saunas, steam rooms, plunge pools and two wonderfully relaxing infinity pools looking out over the Arabian Gulf. Map 3 C1 20

## Cleopatra's Spa

Wafi Pyramids, Oud Metha

04 324 7700
www.waficity.com

Cleopatra's Spa may not have the grand entrance that some hotel spas share, but what it lacks in ostentation it makes up for in occasion. The relaxation area is an ancient Egyptian affair with drapes, silk cushions and majlis-style seats. The spa menu should satisfy all, with massages and facials, body wraps and anti-ageing treatments. The big bonus is that if you book a package you get a pool pass that allows you to float around the 'lazy river' in the tree-shaded pool area. Map 5 B4 21

## Elche

Behind Jumeirah Plaza, Jumeira

04 349 4942
www.elche.ae

Elche utilises the healing potential of herbs, fruit and flowers in its modern scientific methods. Its skincare products are refreshingly fragrant and have a regenerative effect. Set in a walled garden this elegant retreat is warm and peaceful, with the entire experience tailored to the individual. Not only are you given an in-depth analysis by one of the professional therapists, but you will also receive a client evaluation at the end of your treatment and can even have your makeup done by a professional. Map 4 E1 16

### Givenchy Spa
04 315 2140

One&Only Royal Mirage, Al Sufouh    www.oneandonlyresorts.com

The emphasis in this serene setting is on understated decor, with plenty of neutral colours and natural light. The relaxation room is a haven of tranquillity and an ideal spot to savour the sensations after your treatment. Its speciality is the 'canyon love stone therapy', an energy-balancing massage using warm and cool stones. The moonlight-charged stones are placed on specific points around the body, and then used to massage the skin. Only Givenchy products are used in this spa   Map 3 E1 14

### The Haven
04 345 6770

Near Jumeira Mosque, 332-5b Street, Jumeira

Mesmerising scents, earthy decor and gentle background music will guide you into a relaxed state the moment you enter this converted two-storey villa. There are none of the trappings of a hotel spa, but The Haven offers a wide range of treatments including Thai yoga massage, ayurvedic treatments, reflexology, aromatherapy and yoga. The popular hot stone massage is also available. Map 4 F1 25

### The Health Club & Spa at Shangri-La    04 405 2441
Shangri-La Hotel, Sheikh Zayed Road    www.shangri-la.com

This spa offers a holistic approach to healing, featuring traditional Asian treatments. The signature 'chi balance' massage is 50 minutes of blissful stimulation and relaxation. The health club includes a rooftop pool, tennis courts, a squash court and a gym. Relaxation facilities are extensive, with a salon and barber, juice bar and boutique completing the package. Surroundings are minimalist, and the communal areas lean more towards fitness club than spa.    Map 7 A2 26

### LeSpa    04 428 7888
The Palace – The Old Town    www.sofitel.com

Two-floor LeSpa is all about beauty and relaxation. Within the 800 sq m space there are separate areas for men and women to enjoy massage, a tanning salon, a hammam, outdoor heated pool and sauna. Monsoon showers and hydrobaths wash away any remaining stress. LeSpa's French origins mean beauty treatments come with Lancôme products. There are consultants available for personal programmes.    Map 4 D3

### Oriental Hammam    04 315 2130
One&Only Royal Mirage, Al Sufouh    www.oneandonlyresorts.com

This is the ultimate in Arabian luxury. The surroundings are elegant but not overly opulent, with a warm traditional feel. The hammam and spa is an impressive area with mosaic-covered arches and intricate carvings on the high domes. The 50 minute treatment involves being bathed, steamed, washed with black soap, vigorously scrubbed and massaged on a hot marble table. This sounds invasive but manages somehow to be wonderfully invigorating. Map 4 E1 24

## Taj Spa
04 211 3101
Taj Palace Hotel, Deira                    www.tajpalacedubai.com

This is a relaxing and tranquil spa with a romantic atmosphere. The therapists concentrate on the body as well as the mind and methods are based on the ancient science of ayurveda (fused with modern technology). The changing rooms have a sauna and steam room, while the relaxation area is spacious and blessed with sink-in sofas and armchairs. Map 5 D3 27

## Talise Spa
04 366 6818
Madinat Jumeirah, Umm Suqeim              www.jumeirah.com

Attentive staff greet you and immediately whisk you away to the changing rooms. Before or after your treatment you can enjoy the spa's other facilities including sauna, steam rooms and plunge pools. The treatment list is one of the most extensive in Dubai, ranging from traditional massages to more unusual options such as flower therapy. Map 3 B1 28

## Willow Stream Spa & Health Club
04 311 8800
Fairmont Dubai, Sheikh Zayed Road          www.fairmont.com

In keeping with the eclectic decor of The Fairmont, Willow Stream is decorated in a luxurious greco-roman style. There is a selection of top-to-toe spa and beauty treatments using Aromatherapy Associates product lines. Before or after your treatment you can use the fitness centre, the outdoor swimming pools or simply relax with a herbal tea. Map 7 E2 29

# Shopping

Shopping

# With souks, boutiques and mammoth malls at every turn, you won't have any problems spending those dirhams.

Dubai provides innumerable opportunities to indulge in a spot of retail therapy. The city is either a shopaholic's dream or nightmare – depending on who's paying the bill. The rapid development that the city continues to experience is inextricably linked to shopping, and with each new development comes a new mall. The Dubai Shopping Festival (p.38), a month dedicated to consumerism, has taken place annually for more than 10 years.

Shopping in Dubai revolves around the malls, both big and small (see p.156), but it is also well worth checking out the ever-expanding number of independent shops (p.144), as there are some real gems. Practicality plays a large part in mall culture, and during the hotter months they are oases of cool in the sweltering city – somewhere to walk, shop, eat and be entertained – where you can escape the soaring heat for a few hours. From the smaller community malls

## Buyer Beware

**Traps for the unwary do exist in Dubai. Some international stores sell items at far more expensive prices than in their country of origin. You can even see the original price tags. The mark up can be as high as 30% so keep a look out.**

Saks Fifth Avenue

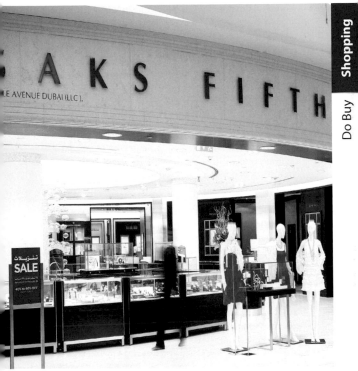

dotted around the city, mostly in Jumeira (p.151), to the mega malls that have changed the skyline, shopping opportunities abound. And with most shops open until 22:00 every night, there's enough time to browse. The popularity of the malls is evident by the crowds that they pull, particularly at the weekends. It takes a brave and dedicated shopper to tackle them on a Friday evening. While average prices for most items are comparable to elsewhere in the world, there are not many places that can beat Dubai's range and frequency of sales. Electronics can be cheaper than the UK or US and Dubai is the world's leading re-exporter of gold.

For most items there is enough choice to find something to fit any budget, from the streets of Karama (p.148) with its fake designer goods, to the shops in the malls (p.156) that sell the real thing.

# Independent Shops

Dubai's independent scene is blossoming. Individual stores and boutiques are opening, predominantly in converted villas, all over the city. Beach Road (p.151) in Jumeira is one of the most popular destinations.

One of the best independent clothes shops, Five Green (04 336 4100; www.fivegreen.com), can be found behind Garden Home Building on Oud Metha Road. It's the place to go for cutting-edge fashion and art. Street chic jeans, printed T-shirts, shirts and trainers from labels including Paul Frank, GSUS and Boxfresh, mixed with creations from Dubai-based designers. Five Green also plays host to a number of exhibitions throughout the year from both home-grown and international talent. Its sister shop, Heaven's Playground, can be found in Wafi Mall (p.167).

Fabindia (04 398 9633; www.fabindia.com) has one of only two branches outside India in Dubai. A riot of bright colours and subtle hues, the clothing ranges for men and women combine Indian and western styles. The hand-crafted fabrics, including soft furnishings, table cloths and cushion covers, will add an ethnic touch to your home. Those looking for home accessories should consider THE One (04 345 6687) on Beach Road. A long-time favourite of Dubaians, it sells contemporary furniture, as well as more unusual one-off pieces that are often elaborate and rather over the top. Its cafe (p.213) is a great spot for a break while trawling Beach Road. Italian leather furniture maker Natuzzi (04 338 0777) has its largest international branch on Sheikh Zayed Road, between Interchange Two and Three.

Contemporary Arabian prints can be found at Gallery One, which has branches in Mall of the Emirates (p.162) and Souk Madinat Jumeirah (p.165). The boho enclave of The Courtyard (p.150) in Al Quoz has funkier furniture and accessories amid its art galleries.

## Mall Eats

Dubai has some fantastic cafes and restaurants in its malls. Lime Tree Café (p.213) at Ibn Battuta, Apres (p.240) and Almaz by Momo (p.236) at Mall of the Emirates, Noodle House (p.229) in Emirates Towers and Shoo Fee Ma Fee (p.238) at Souk Madinat Jumeirah should get you ready for more retail.

## Hotspots

**From the genuine fakes of Karama to the boutiques of Beach Road, there's plenty of action away from the malls.**

## Al Faheidi Street, Bur Dubai

Al Faheidi Street is part of the commercial area that runs from Bastakiya (p.58) all the way to Shindagha and takes in Dubai Museum (p.59). A great place to wander round in the cooler evenings, it's perfect for a bit of local colour and some great shopping. This area has a good range of inexpensive places to eat, including some fantastic vegetarian restaurants near the museum, as well as various outlets at the nearby Astoria (04 353 4300, www.astamb.com) and Ambassador (04 393 9444, www.astamb.com) hotels.

At the heart of Bur Dubai's traditional shopping area, and bordering the Textile Souk (p.154), Al Faheidi Street is home to Dubai's electronics souk. This area is always busy but it really comes to life at night – if you're not sure if you're in the right place, just head for the neon lights. Prices are negotiable and competitive but the vendors know the value of what they're selling. Don't make your purchases at the first shop you go into; rather take the time to look around at the range and prices available. Although goods are often cheaper here, if you are making a big purchase it may be worth it to pay that little bit extra and buy from a major retailer, so that you have more security if something goes wrong. Map 5 C1 🔟

Clockwise from top left: Al Faheidi Street, Karama Market, Al Dhiyafah Street

# Karama

Karama is one of the older residential districts in Dubai, and it has a big shopping area that is one of the best places to find a bargain. The best spot is the Karama Complex, a long street running through the middle of the district. It is lined by veranda-covered shops on both sides. The area is best known for bargain clothing, sports goods, gifts and souvenirs, and it is easy to find 'quality' goods. While you wander round you will quickly become aware of the reason for Karama's popularity (and notoriety), as you will be offered 'copy' watches and handbags at every shop.

If you show any interest you will be whisked into a back room to view the goods – if you have a specific model in mind, ask and they may be able to get it for you. If you're not interested, a simple 'no thank you' will suffice, or even just ignore the vendor completely – it may seem rude, but sometimes it's the only way to cope with the incessant invitations to view 'copy watches, copy bags'. Two of the most popular shops are Blue Marine and Green Eye, while the imaginatively named Asda is around the corner, and offers high quality handbags and accessories crammed into two floors. It's pretty claustrophobic but the range is excellent.

There's a huge range of T-shirts, shoes, shorts and sunglasses at very reasonable prices in Karama. There are several shops selling gifts and souvenirs, from toy camels to mosque alarm clocks and stuffed scorpions to pashminas. Gifts Tent (04 335 4416) is one of the larger outlets and has a wide range, including every colour of pashmina imaginable. The salesmen are happy to take most of them out so you can find exactly the right shade. With loads of small, inexpensive restaurants serving a range of cuisines, you won't go hungry while pounding the streets of Karama. Try Chef Lanka (p.187), Aryaas (p.185) or Saravana Bhavan (p.188). Map 5 B2 **2**

# Satwa

This area, primarily arranged around four streets, is great for fabric and tailoring (p.173), so, if you want a suit head there early in your trip to get measured. After around a week you can have a new, custom-made outfit ready. The pick of the fabric shops is Deepaks (04 344 8836), which has an impressive range, reasonable prices and helpful staff. Shop around, because whatever you are looking for there's bound to be more than one outlet selling it, and prices vary. If you don't fancy the souks, Satwa is also a great place to pick up some tacky souvenirs; from stuffed camels to glass models of the Burj Al Arab, it's all here – without the pushy vendors.

Al Dhiyafah Street is a great place for an evening stroll. There's an eclectic mix of shops and fast food outlets but, for some reason, there is a fairly high shop turnover so don't count on finding the same outlets twice. Al Mallah (p.223), the popular Lebanese restaurant recognisable by its green umbrellas and neon lighting, is highly recommended for delicious and authentic local food including the best falafel in Dubai, if not the world.

Nearby Rydges Plaza Hotel has a number of popular, licensed bars and restaurants including Cactus Cantina, Il Rustico (p.224) and Aussie Legends (p.225). Map 4 E2 **3**

# Sheikh Zayed Road

More than just the highway connecting Abu Dhabi and Dubai, Sheikh Zayed Road, between the Trade Centre and Jebel Ali, is rapidly developing into the city's largest shopping district. The area is a mixture of industrial and retail units which, due to the size and nature of the buildings, house some of the city's larger independent stores.

At the Trade Centre end, the highway is flanked by some of Dubai's tallest buildings. While they are interesting to look at in themselves, it is worth checking out what is happening at ground level. On the left as you travel in the direction of Abu Dhabi are Emirates Towers (home to The Boulevard – see p.156), a number of sports shops, while on the right are a number of cafes and fastfood outlets.

The left-hand side of the stretch between Interchange One (Defence Roundabout) and Interchange Two (Safa Park) is home to Emaar's new Downtown district and the Burj Dubai (p.92). The massive Dubai Mall is scheduled to open in late 2008 – keep an eye on www.thedubaimall.com.

After Interchange Two, the right-hand side of the road is residential while on the left-hand side there are a number of retail outlets and car dealerships. Behind the Pepsi factory is an outlet called Safita (04 339 3230), which sells wooden Indian furniture – it has a decent selection and their prices are better than most. For the sporty, there's Wolfi's Bike Shop (04 339 4453). The area between Interchanges Three and Four looks, at first glance, to be dominated by industrial units but there are some real gems waiting to be discovered. The Courtyard (www.courtyard-uae.com), one street back from the main road near the Spinneys warehouse, is home to a collection of interesting shops and galleries, including Total Arts (04 347 5050), in a very tasteful setting. The Gold & Diamond Park, right by Interchange Four, has much of the choice of the Gold Souk (p.153), but you can browse in air-conditioned comfort. Map 7 B2 **4**

# Beach Road, Jumeira

It might appear to be the centre of cosmetic surgery but a drive along Beach Road offers some good shopping too, especially if independent boutiques are your bag.

Town Centre (04 344 0111), next to Mercato (p.164), has several cafes, including Café Céramique where you can customise a piece of pottery. Its shops include Heat Waves (for beachwear), DKNY and a large branch of Paris Gallery. Further towards Satwa and opposite Jumeira mosque is Palm Strip (04 346 1462). Upmarket boutiques dominate, but you'll also find NBar (04 346 1100), a walk-in nail bar, several restaurants and an internet cafe. Try the enchanting Lola et Moi (04 345 4774) for children's fashion and accessories. For grown-up fashion head to Village Mall (p.166) where you'll find chic boutiques including S*uce. This fashion and lifestyle hotspot is bringing international names such as See by Chloe to Dubai's label-hungry shoppers. Try Luxecouture (04 344 7933), also at Village Mall, if luxury labels are on the shopping list. Nearby Ayesha Depala (04 337 6435; www. ayeshadepala.com) is a darling on the city's style scene. Its dresses are renowned for intricate beading and mixing traditional Indian design with haute couture. Map 4 E1 **5**

# Souks & Markets

**If you want to add a slice of cultural indulgence to your shopping list, head to the souks where you'll find bargains amid the bustle.**

There are a number of souks and markets in Dubai. The souks are the traditional trading areas, some more formally demarcated than others. In keeping with tradition, bargaining is expected and cash is the best negotiating tool.

The Gold, Spice and Textile Souks line either side of the creek, but parking is limited, so if possible it is better to go to these areas by taxi or, if you are visiting all three, park on one side of the creek and take an abra (p.45) to the other side.

Markets are growing in popularity. They are usually based around crafts and are often seasonal but frequency and quality are improving. The Marina Market (p.155) is on every weekend during the cooler months, and Bastaflea, a market near the XVA Gallery (p.61), has recently started up on Saturdays between 10:00 and 19:00. Both are great launch pads for local talents, with artists, jewellers and other crafty types displaying their wares. Admission is free and these markets are a good chance to meet residents, buy some unique keepsakes then enjoy the nearby cafes such as Chandelier (p.197) and Basta Art Café (p.185).

Global Village (www.globalvillage.ae), on the Emirates Road (follow the brown signs from Sheikh Zayed Road), is a huge collection of stalls, food and entertainment from all over the world. It runs from December to March and is a good spot to pick up everything from Chinese lanterns to honey from Yemen. Organised by country, you can spend hours exploring the wares before eating truly international food, including local Dubai favourite Ravi's (p.224) and Krispy Kreme donuts. Just don't overdo dinner before getting on the fairground rides. Open 16:00 to midnight Saturday to Wednesday, and until 01:00 on Thursday and Friday. Entrance costs Dhs.5 and is free for children under 2 years old.

# Gold Souk

This is Dubai's best-known souk and a must-do for every visitor. It's a good place to buy customised jewellery for unique souvenirs and gifts at a reasonable price.

On the Deira side of the creek, the meandering lanes are lined with shops selling gold, silver, pearls and precious stones. These can be bought as they are or in a variety of settings so this is definitely a place to try your bargaining skills – but don't expect a massive discount. Gold is sold by weight according to the daily international price and so will be much the same as in the shops in malls – the price of the workmanship is where you will have more bargaining power. Most of the outlets operate split shifts, so try not to visit between 13:00 and 16:00 as many will be closed.

The Gold Souk is always busy, and it is shaded, but there is added sparkle when you visit in the evenings as the lights reflect on the gold and gems. If you are more interested in buying than enjoying the souk experience, the Gold & Diamond Park (www.goldanddiamondpark.com), by

Interchange Four on Sheikh Zayed Road. There are branches of many of the outlets that are also found in the Gold Souk but here they are quieter. The mall is air conditioned and there's a small cafe. Map 5 C1 🖸

# Spice Souk

With its narrow streets and exotic aromas, a wander through the Spice Souk, next to the Gold Souk, is a great way to get a feel for the way the city used to be. Most of the stalls sell the same ranges and the vendors are usually happy to advise on the types of spices and their uses. You may even be able to pick up some saffron at a bargain price. The shops operate split shifts, but there is more bustle in the evenings. Map 5 C1 🖸

# Textile Souk

The Textile Souk in Bur Dubai is stocked with every fabric and colour imaginable. The textiles are imported from all over the world, with many of the more elaborate coming from the subcontinent and the far east. There are silks and satins in an amazing array of colours and patterns, velvets and intricately embroidered fabrics; basic cottons can sometimes be harder to find but you can always try Satwa (p.149). Prices are negotiable and there are often sales, particularly around the major holidays of Eid and Diwali, and the shopping festivals. It is worth having a look in a few shops before parting with your cash as they may have different stock and at better prices. The mornings tend to be a more relaxed time to browse.

Meena Bazaar (04 353 9304) is the shop that most taxi drivers head for if you ask for the Textile Souk. It has an

impressive selection of fabrics but prepare to haggle. Rivoli
(04 335 0075) has a range of textiles for men on the ground
floor and for women upstairs. The assistants are keen to offer
the 'best discount', but it is always worth bartering to see if
the price will drop further. Map 5 C1

## Marina Market

050 244 5795
www.marinamarket.ae

Marina Walk, Dubai Marina

Dubai's first real outdoor market. Many local artists display
their talents so you might pick up a nice canvas or watercolour
from an up and coming star for a rock bottom price. The
jewellery is particularly popular, with handmade pieces selling
fast, and there are prints, cakes and kids' toys. It is open on
Fridays and Saturdays during the cooler months. Things get
started at 11:00 and wind up around 19:00. Map 2 D2

# Shopping Malls

**More than merely shopping destinations, Dubai's malls are epicentres of activity, with eating, drinking and even skiing on offer.**

### The Boulevard

04 319 8999

Emirates Towers — www.jumeirahemiratestowers.com

The Boulevard houses some of Dubai's most exclusive boutiques and many popular restaurants and bars, including Cartier, Gucci and Yves Saint Laurent. Boutique 1 (04 330 4555, www.boutique1.com) is a favourite of Dubai fashionistas, stocking Stella McCartney, Alexander McQueen, Prada and Jimmy Choo shoes. There's even a stylish cafe where you can ponder your next purchase. Close by is new store Ounass (04 3300 617), another essential stop off for queens of cool; Diane von Furstenburg, Marchesa and Alberta Ferriti are all on offer, with pieces hanging next to work by Emirati artists. If you're into more than shopping, there's also a health club and 1847 (p.134), a men-only spa. Should you need a drink after all that therapy, retail or otherwise, then a cocktail at Scarlett's (p.233) or a glass of fine wine at The Agency (04 330 0000) should take the edge off the impending credit card bill. The Noodle House (p.229) is also licensed and does a mean martini to wash down your bakmi goreng.

This is one of the first malls in Dubai to introduce paid parking (Dhs.10 per hour), but if you're worried about that then this probably isn't the place for you. Map 7 D3 **10**

## BurJuman

Trade Centre Road, Bur Dubai

04 352 0222
www.burjuman.com

BurJuman is a firm favourite in Dubai, and has always been renowned for its blend of designer and high-street brands (Mango and Next), attracting many a well-heeled shopper. The newer expanded area, anchored by legendary New York store Saks Fifth Avenue, has attracted even more designer names, and there are other outlets exclusive to the mall, such as Shanhai Tang, Valentino and Hermes. The original area houses many famous brands such as Gap, Polo Ralph Lauren, Whistles and Escada, as well as some interesting smaller shops.

The outlets within BurJuman are a mixture of clothing, electronics, home decor and sports goods. There are also branches of Yo! Sushi and Dôme cafe on the ground level.

There are enough designer shops to keep even the most dedicated fashionista happy, including Fendi, Just Cavalli and Christian Dior. For everyday fashion, Massimo Dutti and Zara lead the way. If you are into CDs or DVDs, the independent music shops sell a good range and often have sales. There is a branch of Virgin Megastore for those with mainstream tastes and for ticket sales for local events.

There are two foodcourts and numerous cafes, well arranged for people watching, including the popular Pavillion Gardens on the third floor, and Paul on the ground floor, where you can dine outside during the cooler months. There is a taxi rank outside the mall and plenty of underground parking, but it does get pretty full after 18:00 and at the weekend. Map 5 B2 **11**

### Deira City Centre

04 295 1010

Deira                  www.deiracitycentre.com

A stalwart of Dubai's mall scene, this mall attracts the most cosmopolitan crowd. The three floors offer a huge and diverse range of shops where you can find anything from a postcard to a Persian carpet. There's an 11 screen cinema, a children's entertainment centre, a jewellery court, a textiles court and an area dedicated to local furniture, gifts and souvenirs.

It's all anchored by a huge Carrefour hypermarket, a Debenhams department store, and a large Magrudy's bookshop (beyond the cinema). Many high-street brands are represented, including Gap, Next, Pull and Bear and River Island. A number of designer boutiques can be found mostly on the top floor. The City Gate section (on the same level as car parks P2 and P3) is dominated by electronics retailers.

The mall has two foodcourts: one on the first floor, next to Magic Planet, serving mainly fastfood, and one on the second floor, featuring several good sit-down restaurants. There are a number of coffee houses, including Paul, so you're never far from a caffeine kick. The taxi ranks are in the City Gate section. The traffic queues are notoriously painful, especially at weekends and in the evenings. Map 5 D4 **12**

### VIP Shopping

**Be picked up by a resident shopaholic and taken on a guided tour of Dubai's shopping hotspots. To arrange a tailor-made shopping trip, contact Dubai VIP Services on 04 311 6675 or visit www.dubaivipservice.com**

## Dubai Festival City

04 213 6213

Near Garhoud Bridge, Garhoud      www.dubaifestivalcity.com

Dubai Festival City describes itself as 'a city within a city'. It is a 13 acre retail and entertainment destination a short drive from the airport, set along over 3km of creekside corniche. It offers 600 retail outlets (including 25 flagship stores) and 100 restaurants including 40 alfresco dining options. With five hotels on site there will be over 2,500 hotel rooms available when they are fully open, as well as residential suites if you want to stay longer.

The Festival Waterfront Centre has dramatic water features, performance spaces and many international brands. Most of this bright and airy mall might feel a little empty, but that's just because everyone is in IKEA. With a flagship Toys R Us store, Brit favourite Marks & Spencer and designers such as Marc by Marc Jacobs on offer, it won't be long before other retailers are greeting the crowds.

It's not just shopping though. Grand Cinema and a 10 lane bowling alley are here so this is a place where you can happily spend an entire day before dining. Choose from family favourites at Romano's Macaroni Grill, swanky dim sum joint Yauatcha and everything in between, then relax in one of the licensed bars such as Left Bank. Map 6 C2 **13**

## Dubai Outlet Mall

04 367 9600

Dubai to Al Ain Rd      www.dubaioutletmall.com

In a city where the emphasis is on excess, it is refreshing (not only for the wallet) to find a mall dedicated to saving money. Dubai's first 'outlet' concept mall may be quite a way out of town, but bargain hunters will find it's more than worth the drive. Brands on offer include Marc Jacobs, Tommy Hilfiger, Nike and Monsoon. There are also several restaurants and cafes on site.

### Ibn Battuta Mall

04 362 1900
Sheikh Zayed Road
www.ibnbattutamall.com

Named after 14th century explorer Ibn Battuta, who spent 29 years travelling throughout the Middle East and Asia, the mall is divided into six zones, each based on a region that he visited. The range of outlets is staggering, with most international brands represented. There are several anchor stores, including Debenhams and Géant hypermarket. Shops are loosely grouped: China Court is dedicated to entertainment, with several restaurants and a 21 screen cinema, including the UAE's first IMAX screen. Popular eatery Lime Tree Café (p.213) also has a branch in China Court should you fancy some healthy food in relaxed surroundings. Also here is Finz (04 368 5620), for inexpensive, quality seafood. Nearby is iStyle (04 366 9797) for fans of Apple products. It also does repairs in case you dropped your iPod into the hotel pool. If you're in the market for cheaper electronics then go to Sharaf DG (04 368 5115) where you'll find a huge range of reasonably priced gadgets.

The fashion conscious should head for India Court for the likes of Fitz & Simons, H&M, River Island, Topshop and popular independent boutique Ginger & Lace. Persia Court is styled as the lifestyle area, anchored by Debenhams – when you get to Starbucks, make sure you look up to see the ceiling detail. The

Ibn Battuta Mall

foodcourts are at either end of the mall. To reward the kids for trailing round after you, there's a Fun City in Tunisia Court. The taxi points are by the entrance to each court. Map 2 A2 **15**

## Lamcy Plaza
04 335 9999

Near EPPCO HQ, Oud Metha                 www.lamcyplaza.com

Home to five floors of open-plan shopping, with a wide range of outlets, Lamcy is consistently popular. The layout is somewhat confusing but many weird and wonderful shops can be found. Look out for the feng shui store near the foodcourt on the ground floor and Daiso, a Japanese shop with most items costing just Dhs.5. Parking is limited but Lamcy offers a unique service to combat it; if you have to park further away, look out for a red people carrier with Lamcy written on it – it offers a pick-up and drop-off service to the mall. Map 5 B3 **16**

## Mall Of The Emirates
04 409 9000

Interchange Four, Umm Suqeim    www.malloftheemirates.com
You will need to grab a map as you go in, and if you see a
shop that you want to go into, don't put it off until later – it's
far too big to go back. Mall of the Emirates is more than a
mall, it's a lifestyle destination. It houses the indoor ski slope
(Ski Dubai, see p.97), the Kempinski Mall of the Emirates Hotel
and the Dubai Community Theatre & Arts Centre (p.246).

There are more than 400 outlets selling everything from
forks to high fashion. The mall is anchored by Carrefour
hypermarket, Dubai's largest branch of Debenhams (p.168),
Harvey Nichols (p.168) and Centrepoint, which is home to
Baby Shop, Home Centre, Lifestyle, Shoemart and Splash.
There is also a Cinestar cinema where you can treat yourself to
a film in Gold Class, which means enormous leather armchairs
and waiter service throughout. Nearby, the sizeable Magic
Planet includes a bowling alley, and a myriad of games and
rides. Label devotees should head for Via Rodeo (04 340 5559)
to get their fix of designer labels such as Burberry, Dolce &
Gabanna, Salvatore Ferragamo, Tod's and Versace. If you're
more into street chic, there are two H&M stores, a branch of
Reiss, a large Zara shop and the ever popular Massimo Dutti,
as well as Phat Farm, the New York clothing line that will add
a bit of bling to your wardrobe. Those looking for accessories
and jewellery will love Boom & Mellow. Sporty types should
head straight to GO Sport, near the bottom of the Ski Dubai
slope, for all-season apparel.

For entertainment Virgin Megastore has a bookshop and
many international magazines alongside CDs, DVDs, mobile

Clockwise from top left: Deira City Centre, Mall Of The Emirates, BurJuman, Wafi Mall

phones and computers. You'll also find a range of Apple products and accessories.

You'll need to keep your energy up so it's fortunate there is a wide range of dining options, from the Swiss chalet feel of Après (p.240) to any number of decent cafes. Map 3 B3 **17**

## Mercato                                              04 344 4161
Beach Road, Jumeira          www.mercatoshoppingmall.com

Mercato is the largest mall in Jumeira, with more than 90 shops, restaurants, cafes and a cinema. As you drive along Beach Road, the renaissance-style architecture really makes Mercato stand out, and, once inside, the huge glass roof provides a lot of natural light and enhances the Mediterranean feel.

The mall is anchored by Spinneys, a large Virgin Megastore (which has a decent book department) and a new Gap outlet. There is a good mix of designer boutiques and high-street brands in the mall, and shops range from the reasonably priced Pull and Bear to the more exclusive Hugo Boss; there's even a shop dedicated to Barbie. For fashion try Topshop, Next, Massimo Dutti and Mango.

The layout is more interesting than many of the malls and it's worth investigating the 'lanes' so you don't miss anything. There is a foodcourt and a number of cafes and restaurants, including Paul, a French cafe renowned for its patisserie, and Bella Donna, an Italian restaurant where you can dine alfresco. The cinema and large Fun City play area near the foodcourt should keep most of the family occupied. Map 4 D1 **18**

## Souk Al Bahar

Downtown Burj Dubai          www.theoldtownisland.com

Souk Al Bahar is Downtown Burj Dubai's answer to Souk Madinat Jumeirah – albeit on a smaller, more manageable and more exclusive scale. Shops include upscale deli Dean & Deluca, vogue swimwear chain Vilbrequin and ladies' boutique Samsaara. At one end a huge window affords shoppers a view of the world's tallest building, while cafes and restaurants provide pleasant waterside dining. Map 4 D3 **19**

## Souk Madinat Jumeirah          04 366 8888

Umm Suqeim          www.madinatjumeirah.com/shopping

Souk Madinat Jumeirah is a recreation of a traditional Middle Eastern marketplace, complete with narrow alleyways, authentic architecture and motorised abras. The blend of outlets is unlike anywhere else in Dubai, with boutique shops, galleries, cafes, restaurants and bars. It is one of Dubai's hotspots, so spend some time wandering through the souk before enjoying an evening out. The layout, in keeping with traditional souks, can be a little confusing. There are location maps throughout and the main features are signposted. If you're really lost, a member of staff will be able to point you in the right direction.

With an emphasis on unique brands, there are a large number of speciality outlets that aren't found anywhere else in Dubai. The souk is home to a concentration of art boutiques, including Gallery One (selling photos with a local flavour) and Mirage Glass. The stalls in the outside areas sell souvenirs, some tasteful and some tacky.

If you're looking for some new holiday clobber, eye-catching but expensive swimming gear can be found at Vilebrequin, Rodeo Drive is good for label hunters or head to Tommy Bahama for some tropical flavour.

There are more than 20 waterfront cafes, bars and restaurants to choose from, including some of Dubai's hottest night spots and you'll find Left Bank (p.241), Shoo Fee Ma Fee (p.238), Jambase (p.241) and Bar Zar (p.240) to name a few. There's also the impressive Madinat Theatre (www.madinattheatre.com) which sees international and regional artists perform everything from ballet to comedy. Map 3 B1 **20**

### Times Square Center

04 341 8020

Sheikh Zayed Road          www.timessquarecenter.ae

This relatively small mall is bright, modern and set to attract bigger crowds as the various outlets open up to the public. Sharaf DG is the big draw with deals on electronics. You'll also find a large Intersport, several home stores and Toys R Us. The Chillout ice lounge (not licensed) is a unique spot to have a sub-zero drink while wearing boots and a coat. In addition to the foodcourt, there is also the world's first Lamborghini Café, Caribou Coffee and Freshies – The Extreme Cafe. The Big Bus Company (p.110) tour stops here too. Map 3 D3 **21**

### Village Mall

04 349 4444

Beach Road, Jumeira          www.thevillagedubai.com

With more of a community feel than many other shopping spots in Dubai, this is one of the more relaxing malls. There are also pampering opportunities for both men and women at Sensasia spa (04 349 8850). Village Mall is also known for its designer boutiques (try Ayesha Depala and S*uce). There are a number of places to eat, including Shakespeare & Co, the Village Kitchen and Tony's New York Deli. Map 4 E1 **22**

## Wafi Mall

04 324 4555

Wafi City, Umm Hurair                                    www.waficity.com

Wafi is possibly Dubai's most exclusive mall and a popular stop for the Big Bus Company (p.110) tour. Part of the Wafi City complex, with its Egyptian theme and designer boutiques, it really stands out – the store directory reads like a who's who in design. Among its most interesting boutiques are Ginger & Lace, Tigerlily and baby and maternity outfit Chocolate & Pickles. For a more urban look, consider Heaven's Playground. Imaginarium, a children's toy shop, has some great traditional toys and even a separate kid-sized door. There's a large Marks & Spencer and a branch of Jashanmal for a break from the likes of Nicole Farhi or Versace.

There are a number of cafes and restaurants, including Italian restaurant Biella, where you can eat in the alfresco dining area. The children's entertainment area, Encounter Zone, is very popular and has age-specific attractions. If you feel the need for pampering, or an evening out, head across to the Pyramids complex where there are some excellent bars and restaurants and a renowned spa (p.135).

Recent additions include the five-star Raffles Dubai hotel (p.50), an underground carpark and 90 new shops, including the largest Topshop in the UAE and popular LA retailer Kitson. Map 5 B4 **23**

## Department Stores

The scope of department stores covers the full shopping spectrum: from the epitome of chic at Saks Fifth Avenue to the functionality of M&S.

### Debenhams
04 294 0011

Various Locations
www.debenhams.com

A stalwart of the British high street, Debenhams has three stores in Dubai: Deira City Centre (p.158), Ibn Battuta (p.160) and Mall of the Emirates (p.162). The branches all stock perfumes and cosmetics, clothing for men, women and children, and homewares. They carry the popular Designers at Debenhams range with diffusion lines from John Rocha, Betty Jackson, Jasper Conran, Matthew Williamson and Ben de Lisi. This is a good shop for swimwear all year round.

### Harvey Nichols
04 409 8888

Mall of the Emirates, Umm Suqeim
www.harveynichols.com

Dubai simply couldn't call itself a luxury destination without its own Harvey Nichols (the largest branch outside of the UK). It contains a large selection of high-rolling fashion, food, beauty and homeware brands, as well as an intimidating selection of sunglasses. Pick up treats by Jimmy Choo, Diane Von Furstenberg, Juicy Couture, Hermes and Sergio Rossi, then head to the top floor for the popular Almaz by Momo (p.236), a restaurant, juice bar and shisha cafe all in one. Map 3 B3 **17**

## Jashanmal

04 324 4800
Wafi Mall, Umm Hurair    www.jashanmal.ae

One of Dubai's original department stores, with branches in Al Ghurair City, Mall of the Emirates and Wafi Mall. Jashanmal is the importer for several brands including Burberry, Clarks shoes and Mexx. With books, cameras, fashion, gifts, housewares, household and kitchen appliances, and luggage, the stores are definitely worth a look. Map 5 B4 **23**

## Marks & Spencer

04 206 6466
Various Locations    www.marksandspencer.com

One of the best known brands in the UK, M&S, as it is known, sells men's, women's and children's clothes and shoes, along with a small selection of food. It is famous for its underwear, as worn by a huge number of women in Britain, and has a reputation for quality. You'll also find more fashion forward lines including Limited Collection and Autograph alongside the traditional styles it has been carrying for years. Branches in Wafi Mall (p.167) and Dubai Festival City (p.159).

## Saks Fifth Avenue

04 351 5551
BurJuman, Bur Dubai    www.saksfifthavenue.com

Anchoring the extension to BurJuman is the second-largest Saks Fifth Avenue outside the US. The name is synonymous with style, elegance, and the good life, encapsulated on two floors of paradise for the label conscious. You'll find designers galore, including Christian Dior, Jean Paul Gaultier, Prada, Agent Provocateur and Tiffany & Co, in addition to a personalised shopping service. Map 5 B2 **11**

# Where To Go For…

## Carpets

Carpets are one of the region's signature items, although they tend to be imported from Iran, Turkey and Pakistan. The price of a piece depends on a number of factors: its origin, the material used, the number of knots, and whether or not it is hand-made. The most expensive carpets are usually those hand-made with silk in Iran. The higher the quality the neater the back, so turn the carpets over – if the pattern is clearly depicted and the knots are all neat, the carpet is of higher quality than those that are indistinct. Try to do some research so that you have a basic idea of what you are looking for before you go, just in case you happen to meet an unscrupulous carpet dealer. Fortunately, most will happily explain the differences between the rugs and share their extensive knowledge.

Ask to see a selection of various carpets and get a feel for the differences between hand-made or machine-made silk, wool or blend carpets. Prices range from a few hundred to tens of thousands of dirhams. It is always worth bargaining to get a better price.

To find the perfect piece head to Fabindia (Al Mankool Road, Bur Dubai, 04 395 9633), the Pride of Kashmir in Souk Madinat Jumeirah (p.165) and Mercato (p.164), or Persian Carpet House (04 332 1161) in the Crowne Plaza (p.47). There's also a good collection of places in Deira – National Iranian Carpets (04 295 0576), Kashmir Gallery (04 222 5271) and Total Arts (04 228 2888) – and in Souk Al Bahar (p.165) in Downtown Burj Dubai.

## Genuine Fakes

Spotted a divine handbag in BurJuman but can't stretch to the hefty price tag? Found a Rolex but have spent all your dirhams? Then get yourself down to Karama (p.148). Granted, you won't find the real thing, but if you're dying for the Chanel logo or a bit of bling then this is the place to go. There are plenty of 'genuine fakes' available if you're willing to put your bargaining hat on.

Even if you're not a label fan then it's possible to pick up a nicely designed handbag made from good quality leather for around Dhs.300. If it has a logo then you'll be able to find it; jeans, sunglasses, bags, wallets, belts, shoes, jewellery and so much more are all on offer. Quality is mixed so be sure to inspect items properly and point out any faults to knock the price down.

As with everything in Karama, the more you buy the better your bargaining power. Unlike some other Middle Eastern countries, the salesmen aren't too pushy, and a firm 'no thank you' should get rid of any unwanted attention.

## Gold

Gold is notably cheaper in the UAE than in western Europe, making it a popular souvenir, and the main attraction for many visitors. Dubai is the world's leading re-exporter of gold and you'll find a jeweller in even the smallest of malls. It is available in 18, 21, 22 and 24 carats and is sold according to the international gold rate. This means that for an identical piece, whether you buy it in Mall of the Emirates (p.162) or in the Gold Souk (p.153) there should be very little difference in

# Going Out

## Dine, Drink, Dance

**With international cuisine, slick bars and big name DJs, Dubai is fast becoming a nightlife hotspot.**

Whether you decide to sample Gordon Ramsay's offerings at Verre (p.195) or kick back with a juice and falafel at Al Mallah (p.223), Dubai's multicultural mix will show you a good time. Aside from hotel fine-dining (some of which is excellent, some of which is overpriced and average), there are great authentic restaurants and laid-back bars to enjoy, not to mention extravagant brunches, dinner cruises and shisha alfresco.

Friday and Saturday nights are the big ones, with international DJs in the clubs and reservations required in the restaurants. However, during the week you'll find drink deals across the city and all manner of dining promotions. See Special Deals (p.183) for more information.

While Dubai doesn't lend itself to pub crawls by foot or evening strolls around restaurant districts, venues tend to be close together, either within a mall such as Souk Madinat Jumeirah (p.165) or five minutes away by taxi. You'll find upmarket spots in the Marina and Umm Suqeim, more down-to-earth pavement cafes in Satwa, Arabic cuisine in Bur Dubai and cheap curries that will blow your mind and tastebuds in Karama, so it's worth exploring the whole city.

### Drinking

A very common misconception about Dubai is that alcohol is banned. This is far from reality: drinking culture is alive, well and thriving in the city. What you may find odd is the fact that you can't pop into a supermarket and pick up a bottle of wine, or enjoy a beer with dinner at an independent restaurant. In order to get a liquor licence, bars and restaurants need to be attached to a hotel or sports venue. As a result, there are no streets where you can bounce from bar to bar before ending up in a club. Instead, you might find yourself drinking at hotel bars before heading to a nightclub at a nearby resort. Sometimes it may feel strange to emerge from a dark pub into a brightly lit hotel lobby but the convenience factor of taxis outside and good facilities means it doesn't really matter.

## Vegetarian

Despite visions of Middle Eastern cuisine involving meat kebabs and chicken shawarmas, vegetarians will find some delicious local delicacies that will thrill herbivores. Rahib salad, a hot combination of aubergine and tomato makes a great side dish when eating Lebanese food, not to mention tabouleh, fattoush and falafel, all served with fluffy fresh bread.

As a result of the many south-east Asian residents, there are plenty of authentic curries to be tried. Head to

### All Aboard

**Dinner on the creek is a must. From basic dhows to lavish feasts, try Bateaux Dubai (04 399 4994; www. bateauxdubai.com) for luxury or Creek Cruises (04 393 9860; www. creekcruises.com) for the tourist option, complete with belly dancer.**

Karama (p.184) where you'll find restaurants boasting 'veg and non-veg' dishes at insanely low prices. You'll also find thali, which consists of up to 10 small pots of curries, pickles and sauces into which you can dip naan and chapatti or mix with rice. This authentic eating experience will rarely cost you no more than Dhs.12.

# Brunch

Thinking of a bagel and a cup of coffee with friends on a Sunday morning? Think again. Many five-star hotels, including Al Qasr (p.49), Burj Al Arab (p.47), The Park Hyatt (p.50) and Jumeirah Beach, (p.49) put on lavish spreads every Friday afternoon. These all-you-can-eat-and drink affairs often include unlimited champagne and food from all over the world. Of course, such luxury comes at a price – usually around Dhs.350 for the premium options – but when it's too hot to sunbathe or there is something to celebrate they are a fantastic way to spend the day.

If you want to indulge in daytime drinking but don't

## Put That In Your Pipe

It's common to see people relaxing in the evening with a coffee or juice and a shisha pipe. Shisha (also known as hubbly-bubbly or hookah) is a popular method of smoking tobacco with a water-filled pipe. It comes in a variety of flavours, including grape and apple. Some of the best places to try shisha in Dubai are Chandelier (p.197), QD's (p.210) and 360° (p.239).

have the dirhams then head to some of the city's cheaper options: Waxy O'Conner's (p.188) and Double Decker (p.231) put on weekly spreads with booze included.

For a truly unique experience, head to the Iranian Club (www.icd.ae) in Oud Metha where you'll find a vast choice of authentic food and a family atmosphere. Women will need to cover their heads. Other family-friendly brunch choices include More (p.205) and Organic Foods & Cafe (p.223) for tasty salads, pastries and juices from 11:00 to 15:00 every Friday.

## Special Deals

Dig a little deeper, look past the tourist traps and there are many bargains to be had. From free drinks for ladies to seafood buffets, there is a deal out there to suit.

If the idea of brunch appeals but you don't want to give up precious time in the sun, then head to Meridien Village Terrace (p.207) or Yalumba (p.209) where there are midweek deals on all you can eat and drink, often with a different theme depending on the night.

Been out for dinner and a bit strapped for the bar bill? If it's Tuesday and you're female then Dubai's watering holes can help. Head to Lotus One (p.232), Keva (p.220) or Scarlett's (p.233) for free drinks. If it's Friday then Boudoir (p.215) is the place to go for free champagne and cocktails. Making up approximately 75% of Dubai's population, chaps have a harder time getting the freebies but there are a few places that will ease pressure on the spending money. On Fridays Double Decker (p.231) has happy hour all day long, while you can get seven drinks for Dhs.100 at Malecon (p.214).

# Venue Directory

# Bur Dubai & Karama

**Dubai's old business district has the city's most eclectic mix: artsy cafes, dirt-cheap curries and laid-back pubs.**

For a true taste of this multicultural city, head to Karama and Bur Dubai where, among the western pubs and fading hotels, you'll find some culinary gems. One of the cheapest parts of the city, this is the place to find generous helpings of Pakistani fare, piles of fluffy rice, Arabic breads and plenty of spice. Look beyond the lack of aesthetics and instead take advantage of some of the best international food. Arrive with an empty stomach and open mind. There are some great boozy options too.

## Venue Finder

| | | |
|---|---|---|
| Cafe | Basta Art Cafe | p.185 |
| Cafe | XVA Cafe | p.185 |
| Arabic | Bastakiah Nights | p.186 |
| Arabic | Kan Zaman | p.187 |
| Indian | Aryaas | p.185 |
| Indian | Gazebo | p.187 |
| Indian | Saravana Bhavan | p.188 |
| Mexican | Barry's Bench | p.186 |
| Pakistani | Karachi Darbar | p.188 |
| Sri Lankan | Chef Lanka | p.187 |
| Bar | Waxy O'Conner's | p.188 |
| Nightclub | Rock Bottom | p.189 |

# Cafes

### Basta Art Cafe

Bastakiya                                          04 353 5071

The courtyard of the Basta Art Cafe is a quiet sanctuary amid the frenzy of Bastakiya. Sit on majlis-style low cushions, or under one of the white cotton canopies while you look through the rustic menu. Each item features a description of what vitamins and minerals it contains, as well as the calorie count. Works of art have pride of place, with various pieces showcased (and sold) each month. Map 5 C1 **1**

### XVA Cafe

Bastakiya                                          04 353 5383

Find your way through the maze-like alleyways of Bastakiya and you'll discover an unassuming eatery in a courtyard shaded by rustling trees. The cafe's small dishes, fruit juices and teas are Indian-inspired, simple and healthy. Should you go in summer you can lounge in the tapestried and air-conditioned majlis. Perfect for a pre or post gallery bite. XVA is also home to eight guest rooms on the upper floor. Map 5 C1 **1**

# Restaurants

### Aryaas                                        Indian

Kuwait Street                                      04 335 5776

Only an M&M machine and a few pictures disrupt the prison-like austerity of Aryaas, but it's clear the aim is to impress with dirt-cheap 100% vegetarian food rather than decor. The plan works. The house speciality is thali: small pots of different flavours into which you dip as much naan bread or rice as you can physically handle. For around Dhs.10 it will provide enough food to leave you grinning and comatose for the afternoon. Map 5 B2 **2**

### Barry's Bench
**Arabian Courtyard Hotel**

Mexican
04 351 6646

Barry's Bench's position in the Arabian Courtyard Hotel affords two things: views over the fort of Dubai Museum, its dhows, and windtowers – and the all-important drinks licence. You simply can't chow down on top quality Tex-Mex without simultaneously supping a cold cervesa or one of its fantastic margaritas. You might even get a few free tequilas thrown in too. Portions are podgy, though always piping hot and packed with flavour. Map 5 C1 **3**

### Bastakiah Nights
**Near Rulers Court**

Arabic
04 353 7772

There are some meals where mood is almost as important as the food itself. Bastakiah Nights, a haven in the surrounding concrete jungle, combines the two effortlessly. As you enter through heavy wooden doors you are reminded that, despite the glitzy malls and luxurious hotels, this is still very much Arabia. The food is delectable. You can choose from fixed menus or the various a la carte offerings such as lamb stew and stuffed vine leaves. There's no alcohol licence but that shouldn't matter with food this good. Map 5 C1 **1**

## Chef Lanka
Opposite Lulu Supermarket

Sri Lankan
04 335 3050

Chef Lanka is the best chance to try Sri Lankan food in Dubai.
It is a smart, clean little restaurant offering good value and
great tasting food. There is a 'thatched' hut housing the daily
buffet, but authentic dishes, inlcuding a mean nasi goreng,
are cooked to order in the kitchen, allowing you to specify the
spiciness. Alternatively, eat from the buffet for just Dhs.8 at
lunch or Dhs.20 at dinner. Map 5 B2 **4**

## Gazebo
Near Mina Plaza Hotel

Indian
04 359 8555

Diners at Gazebo can assemble an almost infinite number
of personal combinations from the 159 items on the menu.
The 22 breads, 10 desserts and dozens of drinks increase
the possibilities further. The shahi bagh, a succulent dish
of chickpeas, nuts, raisins with a mint flavoured dressing, is
highly recommended. Map 5 B2 **5**

## Kan Zaman
Heritage & Diving Village

Arabic
04 393 9913

With some of the best night views of the creek, Kan Zaman
offers an excellent Arabic menu and a rare chance to try some
Emirati dishes. Mezze and mains are on offer as are traditional
dishes from the UAE and local breads served with either
honey and dates or cheese. There is seating available inside,
but the waterfront views outside are what draws the crowds.
Map 5 C1 **6**

### Karachi Darbar

Karama Shopping Centre

Pakistani

04 267 3131

This popular chain is a great place to find a new favourite dish. If the weather is kind then sit outside. The simple decor, plain menus, and utilitarian settings may not pull visitors in off the street, but the no-nonsense but friendly service, the range of tasty food and the generous portions make this exceptional value. Map 5 B2 **7**

### Saravana Bhavan

Karama Park Square

04 334 5252

Taking its name from the famous and much-loved hotel Saravana Bhavan in Chennai, India, this unassuming joint is arguably the best of the area's south Indian restaurants. The menu is long enough to keep demanding Indian expatriates interested but it's the thalis that draw big crowds. For around Dhs.10 you can get a plate packed with colour and flavours, dal and chapatti. Fine Indian food doesn't come much cheaper. Map 5 B3 **8**

## Bar

### Waxy O'Conner's

Royal Ascot Hotel

04 352 0900

Love it or hate it, this faux Irish pub serves a purpose. You might be in Dubai for only a few days, but if you're from the British Isles and homesickness strikes then get a taxi to Waxy's. Its legendary weekend brunch (Dhs.65 for five drinks, full breakfast then carvery) pulls in the punters,

Bastakiah Nights

including – allegedly – rapper Fifty Cent when he was in town. While you might not be mixing with high society, you'll have a good time and a hangover to remember.
Map 5 B1 **9**

# Nightclub

### Rock Bottom Cafe
Regent Palace Hotel                                            04 396 3888

If you've had a few drinks and need to either dance it off or top yourself up, this no nonsense club fits the bill. Its legendary for the bullfrog cocktails (a terrifying green mix of top shelf spirits, Red Bull and Blue Caraco) and quality cover bands. You should leave your pretensions at the door. Map 5 B2 **10**

## Deira

It's worth battling the traffic for some of the city's finest fare, including Gordon Ramsay's Verre.

This side of the creek has plenty to offer foodies. Most restaurants are in hotels so you'll find plenty of buffets, stylish surroundings and even a celebrity chef. Then there's the revolving restaurant for a dining room with a view (p.191). With everything from Japanese to German cuisine on the various menus, you certainly won't get bored exploring the options. However, the location can mean some terrible traffic mid-week so factor this into your reservations or head to Deira at the weekend.

### Venue Finder

# Restaurants

**Al Dawaar**                                           International
Hyatt Regency Hotel                                    04 317 2222

While you may think a revolving restaurant is mere kitsch, don't be too hasty in dismissing Al Dawaar. This is a surprisingly sophisticated Arabic buffet restaurant on the 25th floor of the hotel. As you enjoy the cuisine including Japanese and Middle Eastern dishes, the slow revolution (it takes one hour and 45 minutes to do a complete turn) gives you an interesting window on this side of town. Map 5 D1 **11**

**Ashiana**                                                  Indian
Sheraton Dubai Creek Hotel                             04 207 1733

With empire-inspired decor and a traditional band playing authentic tunes every night, Ashiana celebrates India's colonial era. Cosy booths around the walls are the seats of choice, unless you're in a large group. The staff deserve a special mention for their swift and friendly service. Map 5 C2 **12**

**Bamboo Lagoon**                                       Far Eastern
JW Marriott Hotel                                      04 262 4444

With a little bridge and a big crocodile, you won't forget the decor in a hurry. The food is memorable too: there's sushi, tempura, teriyaki, curries, steaks, stir-fries, grills, seafood, rice and noodle dishes. All are equally tempting and so wonderfully presented that you'll wish you hadn't eaten that big lunch. At 21:00 a band takes to the stage and grass-

skirted singers serenade diners with low-key renditions of tropical Polynesian tunes and entertaining cover versions.
Map 5 D3 **13**

## Glasshouse
Hilton Dubai Creek

European
04 227 1111

Get a taste of the Mediterranean at this chic brasserie with glass walls, dark woods, tasteful colours, and Mondrian-style paintings. The menu provides contemporary dishes with a touch of flair. A Friday brunch is available with free-flowing drink options, including champagne. Map 5 C2 **13**

## Hofbrauhaus
JW Marriott

German
04 262 4444

From the sauerkraut to the white sausage with sweet mustard, everything here is authentically Bavarian. Add in the beer hall decor, traditional garb for the staff and accordion music and you have a recipe for a fun night out. Several German beers are on tap, along with a full selection of wines and spirits. Map 5 D3 **14**

## JW's Steakhouse
JW Marriott

Steakhouse
04 262 4444

Set in an intimate, secluded part of the hotel, JW's Steakhouse makes its intentions clear the moment you walk through the door when chefs can be seen cleaving huge chunks of meat in the open kitchen. Once you are shown to your stately leather armchair, a huge menu offering an impressive range of steak and seafood awaits. Map 5 D3 **14**

Clockwise from top left: Glasshouse, The China Club, Miyako

### Miyako
Hyatt Regency Hotel

Japanese

04 317 2222

Miyako is filled with Japanese patrons, night after night, all enjoying astoundingly good food. Those in the know and business people wanting to close important deals also frequent this excellent eatery. It's certainly not Dubai's cheapest Japanese option, but the standard of food, decor and impeccable service ensure most leave feeling they got what they paid for and more. Map 5 D1 **11**

### Spice Island
Renaissance Hotel

International

04 262 5555

When it comes to choice, it doesn't come much wider than Spice Island. Diners of every taste, from Italian to Mongolian, will be satisfied by the mouthwateringly varied buffet. The Friday and Saturday brunch is also hugely popular with families (it is smoke-free and includes a kid's area with balloons and face painting) and those looking for some hangover grease. Map 5 D2 **15**

### The China Club
SAS Radisson Dubai Creek

Chinese

04 205 7333

The China Club serves far eastern delights in a slick, formal setting, where crisp table linen and subtle Asian decor set the tone, and attentive waiters do the rest. The extensive menu (which includes an impressive selection of carefully planned set menus) features exotic dishes, alongside more traditional Chinese dishes (dumplings, spring rolls and dim sum). Map 5 C2 **16**

## The Fish Market

Seafood

SAS Radisson Dubai Creek

04 205 7333

Accompanied by a member of staff clad in plastic gloves and clutching a wicker shopping basket, you can select fresh fish then request the style of cooking. While you wait for your tailor-made dinner to arrive you can snack on a bowl of french fries and soak up the creekside view. Map 5 C2 **16**

## Verre

French

Hilton Dubai Creek

04 227 1111

You enter through sleek, sliding glass doors, but your first impressions of the decor – understated dark wood furniture and simple white table linen – may leave you wondering what all the fuss is about. However, Gordon Ramsay is a chef, not an interior designer, and Verre is all about the food. Faultless service and the delightful canapes and between-course treats make this a truly memorable dining experience, albeit an expensive one. Map 5 C2 **14**

# Bar

## Chameleon

Traders Hotel Dubai

04 265 9888

This vibrant cocktail bar has reasonably priced drinks from sophisticated Martinis to signature Chameleon concoctions that may have you licking your lips or climbing the walls. Depending on which night you visit, the music may be provided by a live pianist or a hip DJ, occasionally accompanied by live bongo and saxophone players. Map 5 E3 **17**

# Dubai Marina & Al Sufouh

Home to a crop of the city's best bars and restaurants, New Dubai is at the high-rise heart of the social scene.

Beach views, award-winning restaurants and hip bars make this area an excellent destination for dining and drinking. But leave the flip-flops in the suitcase and go out in style.

## Venue Finder

# Restaurants

### Bussola
Le Meridien Mina Seyahi

Italian
04 399 3333

A Sicilian influence on the menu means the choices are slightly more adventurous than your standard Italian fare, but all are worth your attention. Save room for dessert because the chef's creations are art on a plate. The open-air first-floor veranda serves cocktails and pizza to a backdrop of sparkling sea views and chill-out tunes. Map 2 E1 **18**

### Certo
SAS Radisson Media City

Italian
04 366 9111

Certo is less Mama's home-cooked masterpiece and more suave Italian businessman in a bespoke suit – which is perfectly appropriate given its location in the heart of Dubai Media City. Trendy account execs will feel right at home in this handsome setting with its wood and faux-croc skin panels, chrome and glass. Meanwhile, burnt-out creatives will love the glass-walled wine cellar, where ruby merlots and grassy chardonnays rest on high metal shelves.
Map 2 E2 **19**

### Chandelier
Marina Walk

Lebanese
04 366 3606

Set in the area's heart at Marina Walk, Chandelier has a stylish, modern interior and very pleasant outdoor seating, ideal for enjoying shisha after dinner. The Lebanese fare is inventive, with the menu offering an interesting mix of standard and unique dishes, and a full range of (non-alcoholic) cocktails and juices. Service is renowned as being leisurely, but this is a great place to linger over a meal. Map 2 C2 20

### The Dhow
Seafood

Le Meridien Mina Seyahi
04 399 3333

From the moment you walk down the candlelit path and step aboard this permanently moored traditional dhow you know you're in for a treat. You can choose to dine in the air-conditioned lower deck or go alfresco and enjoy the view of the marina and the ocean from the top deck. The menu focuses heavily on seafood, starting with fresh oysters and a tantalising choice of sushi and sashimi. Map 2 E1 18

### Eauzone
Far Eastern

One&Only Royal Mirage
04 399 9999

One of the most romantic restaurants in Dubai, Eauzone has poolside tables, low lighting and sublime exotic food. The attentive staff, including one of the best sommeliers in town, are happy to explain dishes. The Asian inspired options include sushi, scallops, risotto and Thai prawns but with curve balls such as foie gras thrown in, you'll find surprises with every page of the menu. Map 2 E1 21

### Frankie's
Italian

Oasis Beach Tower
04 399 4311

Co-owned by Frankie Dettori and Marco Pierre White, this new bar and restaurant is a tasty illustration of the burgeoning marina, and a follow up to the pair's London restaurant. Grab a

La Baie

vodka martini and thin-crust pizza in the bar or head into the main restaurant for Italian classics and new favourites such as duck ravioli. With a dark interior, pianist and even a waitress called Babes, this is no one-horse trick. Map 2 C1 22

## Indego
Indian

Grosvenor House
04 399 8888

A suitably stylish match for Grosvenor House, Indego has a cool, low-lit interior with various areas screened off by elegant wooden partitions. The menu offers Indian dishes with a contemporary international twist, such as the wild mushroom biryani that comes with a flaky pastry crust and a side order of dhal. Eat here and you'll see why consultant Vineet Bhatia was the first Indian chef in the world to be awarded a Michelin star. Map 2 D2 23

### La Baie
Ritz Carlton

Seafood
04 399 4000

In Dubai's 24 hectic culture, it's easy to forget how to luxuriate over a meal. La Baie reminds you. If the music doesn't massage away stress, the wine list showcases some stunning tension relievers. With Korean-Japanese and French chefs at the helm, the resulting food is an exciting mix of traditional and imaginative sushi and seafood. Map 2 D1 **24**

### Nineteen
Montgomerie Golf Club

International
04 390 5600

Still need convincing that golf is cool? Head to Nineteen, where slick, pared-back modernism sends members-only fustiness the way of wooden clubs. The restaurant would be pitch black save for a pink back-lit bar, 70s kitsch lampshades, and subtle lights that single out your table. Choose from a perfectly balanced Thai-influenced menu and see the food get better with each course. Map 2 D5 **25**

### Nina
One&Only Royal Mirage

Indian
04 399 9999

Guests already smitten with the One&Only Royal Mirage will fall head over heels in love with Nina. Massive chandeliers and graceful candelabra cast their muted light on faux marble walls and tiled circular arches. Percussive music accompanies conventional Indian main courses flanked by inventive starters and desserts. The staff know the ingredients of each dish and provide diners with time to reflect on the food and the lively atmosphere. Map 2 E1 **21**

## Rhodes Mezzanine
British

Grosvenor House
04 399 8888

Gary Rhodes is a British celebrity chef with vertical hair and a zealous mission to stop Johnny Foreigner carping on about the stodginess of UK cuisine. Mezzanine is not moderately priced, but the food is Michelin quality. The simple menu focuses on modern British classics, such as jam roly-poly, an excellent oxtail cottage pie and pork belly. Parts of the wine list run into four figures, but you can find decent bottles for around Dhs.200. Map 2 D2 **23**

## Tagine
Moroccan

One&Only Royal Mirage
04 399 9999

Beneath ground level, through an enormous wooden door, past a majlis area soaked in rich embroidery and incense smoke you'll find the authentic Tagine. The low-seating and traditonally dressed waiters create a traditional vibe, even if the pastillas, aromatic tagines, spicy kebabs and exotic couscous don't live up to their billing. Map 2 E1 **21**

## The Rupee Room
Indian

Marina Walk
04 390 5755

Occupying a prime spot along popular Marina Walk, the Rupee Room offers a wide selection of north Indian dishes in comfortable and relaxed surroundings. The indoor dining area spills out on to a covered walkway, and a wooden staircase leads to the mezzanine level. Weather permitting, the best tables are those outside, providing good views of the marina and the ocean beyond. Map 2 C2 **20**

# Bars & Pubs

### Bar 44
Grosvenor House                                    04 317 6871

At Bar 44 waiters with waistcoats that match the bar's carperts whizz around with expensive bottles of champagne, a jazz singer swoons impressively at a grand piano, and plumes of (pricey) cigar smoke fills the air. It's best get here early, say 18:00, when the killer view of the snaking marina from the 44th floor can be best enjoyed. Map 2 D2 23

### Barasti
Le Meridien Mina Seyahi                            04 399 3333

Barasti has beachside beds, a downstairs bar and big screens for the all-important big games, along with heaps of casual charm. This laid-back bar is a big expat favourite, loved for its meaty menu, jugs of Pimms and panoramic vistas, not to mention the fact you can turn up in flip-flops or Friday finery depending on your mood. Map 2 E1 18

### Buddha Bar
Grosvenor House                                    04 399 8888

Buddha Bar has the wow factor. From the entrance, a seductively lit corridor leads you past private lounges and tucked-away alcoves, all perfectly decadent places to dine, lounge, and socialise. With the Buddha Bar's famous mix of music, some of the best cocktails in town, and a selection of tasty Asian treats, this is a firm favourite among Dubai's army of socialites. Map 2 D2 23

### Rooftop Lounge & Terrace

One&Only Royal Mirage                          04 399 9999

Clever design and lighting combine with a subtle DJ to make this one of Dubai's finest bars. Rooftop has a superb view of Palm Jumeirah, majlis-style seating, intimate booths with huge cushions and a good menu of cocktails and bottled beers. If you're looking to kick back your heels and relax under the stars there's no better place. Map 2 E1 21

### Tamanya Terrace

Radisson SAS Media City                         04 366 9111

Tamanya Terrace welcomes business visitors, tourists and media locals in a trendy mix of concrete and chrome. From its position on the seventh floor, you get a great view across Dubai Marina and out across Al Sufouh Road. There's a small menu featuring Arabic bites. The corner bar and unobtrusive DJ fit the bill: somewhere to unwind after a long day at the beach. Map 2 E2 19

## Nightclub

### Peppermint

Habtoor Grand                                   04 332 0037

It's easy to mistake this swanky club for a catwalk show so be sure to throw on your glad rags before strutting across the enormous dancefloor. World-famous DJs regularly stop off to entertain the beautiful people so you won't hear anything but cutting-edge tunes. Only open on Fridays. Map 2 D1 28

# Garhoud

**Ethnic variety, creekside vistas and a converted church make this a special part of town.**

Best known for the sprawling Irish Village (p.210) and all the alfresco fun that follows, Garhoud has some outstanding fine dining options to explore. Many hotel restaurants have multiple offerings, including everything from shisha to lobster. Check out the outstanding brunch at Yalumba (p.209) if you're feeling particularly decadent.

## Venue Finder

# Cafe

## More

Near Welcare Hospital                                04 283 0224

Known for its non-boozy brunches, outstanding sandwiches
and imaginative salads, More attracts both fashionable
media types and families. The stylish industrial interior,
speedy service and extensive menu makes it one of the most
popular weekend spots in town. Try the strawberry juice with
balsamic vinegar and the spinach salad with pumpkin and
feta. You won't regret it. Map 6 D1 29

# Restaurants

## Anise                                                International

InterContinental Hotel Festival City                  04 701 1111

Anise is a truly international affair, with chefs from all over the
world manning the kitchen. With the interior created by uber-
cool Asian design group Super Potato, the atmosphere is as
exciting as the food. Live cooking stations feature dishes from
Thailand, China, Italy, Arabia and India, making this a great
stop for a long lunch or lingering dinner, before moving on to
a nearby bar. Map 6 C2 30

## Blue Elephant                                            Thai

Al Bustan Rotana Hotel                                04 282 0000

Walking into The Blue Elephant is like travelling to Thailand
without the hassle of jetlag. While sitting at bamboo tables,
gazing into a lagoon and surrounded by verdant tropical

greenery, the smell of orchids is evocative of exotic far eastern climates. The menu showcases an array of superb Thai food, spiced to your liking, with distinctive oriental ingredients and traditional flavours. Map 5 D4 **31**

### Boardwalk
Dubai Creek Golf & Yacht Club

International
04 295 6000

Positioned on wooden stilts over the creek, Boardwalk offers patrons a spectacular view virtually unmatched in Dubai. The menu is of a comprehensive array of starters, salads, meats, seafood, and vegetarian dishes, as well as desserts. Servings are generous and well presented while the drinks list contains a standard array of wines and beers and a huge selection of cocktails and mocktails. Map 5 C4 **32**

### Café Chic
Le Meridien Dubai

French
04 282 4040

Subtle art deco decor blends with the sound of mellow jazz that fills Café Chic, while comfortable upholstered dining chairs surround each table and signal the restaurant's desire to pamper its guests. The chef provides distinctive treats before your ordered courses and the service is swift and efficient. Some of the best French food in the city, with set menus priced competitively. Map 5 D4 **33**

### Kiku
Le Meridien Dubai

Japanese
04 282 4040

This is one of Dubai's most popular Japanese joints. It is regularly packed with Japanese guests, sushi lovers or

Yalumba

novices looking to expand their cuisine catalogue. The menu offers standard staples such as sushi, sashimi, tempura and teppanyaki alongside some more unusual delicacies. Particularly worth trying are the surprisingly good value set meals. Map 5 D4 [33]

## Meridien Village Terrace

International
Le Meridien Dubai 04 282 4040

Beautifully lit at night, this large space manages to feel intimate for couples but is also perfect for larger groups. Each night there is a different culinary theme: Caribbean, Mexican, BBQ or Arabic. Numerous live-cooking stations, including one serving made-to-order crepes, keep the food wonderfully fresh. The great choice of drinks are replenished with alarming regularity. Map 5 D4 [33]

### Sukothai
Le Meridien Dubai
Thai
04 282 4040

Decked with dark walls and authentic Thai artefacts, this charming restaurant is a perfect venue for a romantic occasion, especially when it's cool enough to dine outside. The menu is extensive, offering Thai favourites including curries (try the red lobster curry) and a good seafood selection. The dishes are impressive if not cheap. Map 5 D4 33

### Thai Kitchen
Park Hyatt Dubai
Thai
04 317 2222

Intertwined around four live-cooking areas where all the ingredients are displayed and prepared, Thai Kitchen is a slick, contemporary dining space. With small, tapas-style portions at reasonable prices, your best bet is to order two or three per person and share. The duck curry is outstanding and the attentive staff will keep the sticky rice coming. Map 5 C4 34

### The Cellar
Aviation Club
International
04 282 9333

Diners enjoy their own space in a well-lit room of soaring arches and unexpected stained glass. The outside terrace is also pleasantly relaxed with just a glimmer, and whisper, of the more raucous Irish Village (p.210) across the pond. Its Saturday brunch, where you order a a la carte, is recommended. The Cellar's international menu has some favourites and some innovations and the wine list, with special bargains on Saturday and Sunday evenings, shows a surprisingly unusual range. Map 6 C1 35

## Traiteur
French

Park Hyatt Dubai
04 602 1234

Having descended from an intimate bar via a dramatic staircase, you'll be struck by the restaurant's soaring ceilings. Traiteur's beautiful open kitchen then provides a great focal point for the French and modern European cuisine. The menu is ordered by ingredient, a flourish typical of this showy restaurant. Head to The Terrace (p.210) afterwards. Map 5 C4 🖼️

## Yalumba
International

Le Meridien Dubai
04 282 4040

Famous for its raucous Friday bubbly buffets, this predominantly Australian restaurant doesn't limit itself to steak. Head there for the Thursday night buffet with unlimited champagne, sushi, stir-fry, seafood, steak and more desserts than you can possibly manage. Wednesdays feature an Aussie barbecue where you can even throw your own shrimps on. Just leave your board shorts at home. Map 5 D4 🖼️

# Bars & Pubs

## Dubliners

Le Meridien Dubai
04 282 4040

This is a cosy, friendly, and lively Irish pub, with a decent outside patio and screens to watch the football. The menu has good pub staples that are fresh, tasty and reasonably priced, including Bailey's cheesecake. There is a good range of beers on tap, including a decent pint of Guinness and an extensive range of cocktails. Map 5 D4 🖼️

## Irish Village

The Aviation Club  04 282 4750

The Irish Village is the nearest thing Dubai has to a beer garden, and the best place to go for fish and chips (complete with Guinness batter) and a pint of the dark stuff. Expect hearty pub food, twinkly lights in the trees and the odd live musician strumming some Ronan Keating. Map 6 C1 **35**

## QD's

Dubai Creek Golf & Yacht Club  04 295 6000

Settle down, drink in hand and enjoy the view of the creek. With the occasional passing abra, the city lights reflecting on the water and an excellent cocktail list, QD's is one of the best spots in town for sundowners. The shisha, live DJ and decent bar snacks don't hurt either. This is a great place in which to escape the frenetic malls and crowded streets. Map 5 C4 **32**

## The Terrace

Park Hyatt  04 602 1234

Sweep through the Park Hyatt's greenery and you'll reach The Terrace. Awash in icy, contemporary white, chrome and wood, the space-age interior extends out through shiny conservatory doors to an awning-adorned terrace. Sprinkled with couches and wooden tables, this gorgeous alfresco spot gazes out over the yachts and the multi-lit creek beyond. The drinks list is lenghty, ranging from lethal absinthe-based shooters to an unusually brief selection of wine and a wealth of whiskies. Map 5 C4 **34**

Clockwise from top left: Blue Elephant, The Cellar, Kiku

# Jumeira

## There's relatively slim pickings in Dubai's most desirable 'hood, but there'll always be Lime Tree Cafe.

Jumeira is a neighbourhood spot best known for Beach Road, which runs the length of the coast. While there are a wealth of malls, boutiques and sandy shores, the options for a big meal out or night on the tiles are limited due to the lack of hotels. However, it's quality not quantity that counts. You can join the well-heeled residents at hidden gem Smiling BKK (p.214), take a Lime Tree Cafe (p.213) salad to the beach or just enjoy some excellent ladies' night freebies at Boudoir (p.215).

After a few mojitos at Malecon (p.214) the Cuban band will have you thinking that you're the greatest dancer in Dubai. For more sophisticated, sushi-fuelled antics, shimmy under the stars at Sho Cho (p.214).

### Venue Finder

# Cafes

## Lime Tree Cafe

Near Jumeira Mosque                    04 349 8498

Set in a converted villa on Beach Road, this impressive cafe has become a Dubai institution. The understated interior features trendy plastic chairs, dark wood tables and lime-green washed walls. With a definite nod towards Mediterranean cuisine, there's plenty of paninis filled with wholesome ingredients, as well as delicious couscous salads, satay kebabs and the best carrot cake in the city. Map 4 E1 **36**

## THE One

Near Jumeira Mosque                    04 342 2499

Tucked away on the first floor of THE One (p.145), this small cafe is decorated in the same elaborate style seen throughout the store. The Thai-influenced menu is limited but imaginative. The freshly squeezed juices, smoothies and coffee are excellent, and the home-made cakes outstanding. With friendly and attentive service, this is a perfect spot for refuelling. Map 4 F1 **37**

# Restaurants

## Johnny Rockets                                American

Opposite Jumeirah Centre                    04 344 7859

If you want a taste of good old America, with a *Back to the Future* movie feel, then Johnny Rockets is the place. This 1950s style diner offers a lively yet casual dining experience, where freshly cooked burgers and fries are washed down with thick milkshakes. To ensure you control the soundtrack, get there early and bag a booth with a jukebox. Map 4 E1 38

### Malecon
Cuban

Dubai Marine Resort & Spa
04 346 1111

Malecon's high turquoise walls, big windows that overlook a glowing lagoon and low lighting creates a sultry Cuban atmosphere that builds up slowly during the course of the evening, helped along by the live music and Salsa dancers. And while the menu isn't massive (the signature paella is the best choice), the clientele is undeniably tasty. Map 4 F1 39

### Smiling BKK
Thai

Al Wasl Road
04 349 6677

This outstanding Thai pad is a rare and beautiful thing: a restaurant that serves great food with a side of good humour. The cheekily named dishes (some are too rude to print) are reasonable at around Dhs.30 but it's the atmosphere that sets Smiling BKK apart. With gossip mag pages for place mats, walls full of photos and ingenious theme nights such as 'sing for your supper', you're guaranteed to leave grinning. Map 4 D2 40

## Bar

### Sho Cho

Dubai Marine Beach Resort & Spa
04 346 1111

Sho Cho is a perfectly fine Japanese restaurant but that's not the real reason the beautiful set flock to its shoreline location.

Sho Cho

The sizeable bar flanked by two alfresco eating areas, and guarded by sharp-eyed waiters, is the real attraction. The tiny dancefloor is a poser's paradise; there's barely room to swing a man in tight jeans. Map 4 F1 39

## Nightclub

### Boudoir

Dubai Marine Beach Resort          04 345 5995

This exclusive spot can be as difficult to get into as a lady's chamber but once you get past the doormen – as long as you are appropriately dressed – you will be treated to a Parisian-style club that's perfect for dangerous liaisons. The regular free drinks for ladies help pack the circular dancefloor. Map 4 F1 39

# Oud Metha & Umm Hurair

This unheralded part of town offers everything from low-key Thai to big name DJs.

Away from the bustle of Sheikh Zayed Road and the Marina's big hotels, this area is always a pleasure for a night out. Choose from high-class glamour at China Moon (p.219), Keva (p.220) and Ginseng (p.219), chilled out dishes at Seville's (p.218) and Lemongrass (p.218) – or dance the night away at Plan B (p.221) or Chi@The Lodge (p.220). For food and fun, you can always opt for loveable dive Jimmy Dix (221). There's plenty of upmarket cuisine on the menu so decide what you fancy and loosen the belt.

## Venue Finder

# Restaurants

### Asha's
Wafi Pyramids

Indian
04 324 4100

Owned by Indian superstar Asha Bhosle, this Dubai favourite offers a memorable dining experience. Decked out in summer colours of reds, yellows, and oranges, the space features beaded curtains, low-level lighting, and intimate booths as well as an inviting terrace. The menu features a few Indian favourites plus a selection of Asha's very own signature dishes picked up on her travels. Map 5 B4 **41**

### Fakhreldine
Movenpick Hotel Bur Dubai

Arabic
04 336 6000

From your first dip into Fakhreldine's creamy hummus to the last crumb of Arabic sweets, the quality is apparent – and the bill less painful than you might expect. The decor is impressive, as is the gyrating belly dancer, making this a restaurant worth dressing up for. Map 5 B3 **42**

### Indochine
Grand Hyatt Dubai

Chinese
04 317 1234

A fusion of exotic flavours awaits at Indochine. Serving a blend of Vietnamese, Thai, Cambodian and Laosian dishes, it offers some exciting and unusual a la carte choices, especially the imaginative salads and soups. The predominantly dark wood and bamboo decor is cleverly counter-balanced by the high ceilings, tall windows and well-spaced tables. Map 5 B4 **43**

### Lemongrass
Near Lamcy Plaza

Thai
04 334 2325

The simple stylish design of Lemongrass reflects its food. The innovative and user-friendly menu offers a typical range of Thai starters, soups, salads, noodles, curries, stir-fries and desserts. For those who can't take the heat, spice levels can be tailored to individual preferences. There's no alcohol, but the refreshing fruit mocktails more than compensate. Map 5 B3 44

### Seville's
Wafi Pyramids

Spanish
04 3247 300

Come here to enjoy the tapas menu, or the well-stocked bar, or both. In the early evening the place is perfect for a candlelit dinner or drink on the alfresco rooftop garden as the live acoustic guitar sets the mood. Later, the atmosphere picks up, the drinks flow and that indefinable Mediterranean magic works its charms. Map 5 B4 41

## Bars

### Carter's
Wafi Pyramids

04 324 4100

Better suited to large, casual groups than intimate couples, Carter's is adept at attracting the singles crowd, who enjoy good drink deals and a genuinely friendly atmosphere. The mellow background music gives way to live soft rock around 22:00, when Carter's evolves from a restaurant into a nightclub. Food is still available until late, but the focus has shifted to the buzzing crowd surrounding the bar. Map 5 B4 41

Fakhreldine

## China Moon Champagne Bar
Raffles Dubai                              04 324 8888

The black tiling, leather armchairs and vast, circular cream sofas make this bar feel plush, but its disco lighting lowers the tone and the steel struts and glass walls have a giant greenhouse feel. It's a place to sip good wines, spirits and fizz, and located on the top floor of Raffles hotel (p.50), the views across town are impressive. Map 5 B4 45

## Ginseng
Wafi Pyramids                              04 324 8200

Ginseng is an ideal place to sip a luscious long drink. The Asian-inspired nibbles are the perfect partner for champagne cocktails, all served in deep red surroundings. There are good

deals on Tuesdays and menu discounts on Mondays. Stop off at Ginseng after shopping at Wafi Mall (p.167) or start your night off there in style. Map 5 B4 **41**

### Keva

Al Nasr Leisureland                                      04 334 4159

This restaurant-lounge will please everyone with its live music, superb cocktails and international cuisine. With curries to sushi and free mojitos for the ladies on Tuesdays, this is the ideal stop off before a night at Chi@The Lodge (p.220) next door. The inventive decor even has fake grass in the ladies' toilets. This new addition won't be under the radar for long. Map 5 B4 **46**

### Vintage

Wafi Pyramids                                           04 324 4100

Vintage is a cheese and wine aficionado's dream. Wines range from the most respectable plonk to a dazzling array of costly vintages, burgundies and champagnes, but despite the exclusive list this feels more like a friendly local than a stuffy wine bar. Fondue nights, on Fridays and Saturdays, offer a bottle of white or red and generous fondue for two for Dhs.145. Map 5 B4 **41**

## Nightclubs

### Chi@The Lodge

Al Nasr Leisureland                                      04 337 9470

The Lodge is always busy with its indoor and outdoor dancefloors, lots of seating and large screens and VIP 'cabanas'. The regular theme nights with fancy dress are popular and this is also home of the legendary 'cheese' nights with DJ Tim Cheddar. If you needed more reasons to go, it's easy to get taxis outside, there's often a shawarma stand in the carpark and entrance is free before 22:30 on most nights. Keep an eye on listings magazines for upcoming events, live music and offers at this fun favourite. Map 5 B3 46

## Jimmy Dix

Movenpick Hotel Bur Dubai                    04 336 8800

A friendly, unpretentious bar and nightclub with a relaxed dress code, Jimmy Dix delivers a good time. The DJ and talented live band always satisfy the crowds, especially on its 'Thursday Thump' weekend party. It also plays host to Laughter Factory comedy nights (p.245). The food is unexpectedly good with a mix of Tex-Mex, grills, burgers, sausage and mash, and crumbles. A jack of all trades and the master of one monstrous hangover. Map 5 B3 42

## Plan B

Wafi Pyramids                    04 324 4100

The VIP room upstairs serves champagne and sushi, but the focus on the floor is on dancing not dining. Aimed at people looking for a relaxed late night hangout (no cover charge or ridiculous drinks prices), Plan B is a refreshing change to Dubai's sometime exclusive nightlife. The music is wide ranging, with happy hour adding to the fervour of Saturday nights. Map 5 B4 41

## Satwa

# Home to Dubai's best street life, finest falafel and a choice of no-nonsense boozers, Satwa is full of flavour.

Mention Satwa to any Dubai resident and they immediately think of food and fabric. This buzzing spot is one of the best places to sample Arabic cuisine with Al Mallah (p.223) and Sidra (p.225) known throughout the city for their falafel and haloumi respectively.

A walk down Al Dhiyafah Street offers plenty of dining choices. Ignore the usual fastfood suspects and you'll find baskets full of fresh bread, fresh juices and cheap prices. Ravi's is a favourite for its late-night butter chicken, while the mezze and kebabs at Pars keep customers coming back. Satwa's authentic treasures are just the thing after a few beers at one of the area's pubs. Don't expect high class or cocktails, but for a pint and the football these places hit the spot.

## Venue Finder

| | | |
|---|---|---|
| Cafe | Organic Foods & Cafe | p.223 |
| Arabic | Al Mallah | p.223 |
| Indian | Coconut Grove | p.223 |
| Iranian | Pars Iranian Kitchen | p.224 |
| Italian | Il Rustico | p.224 |
| Lebanese | Sidra | p.225 |
| Pakistani | Ravi's | p.224 |
| Bar | Aussie Legends | p.225 |
| Bar | Boston Bar | p.225 |

# Cafe

## Organic Foods & Cafe

Near Satwa Roundabout                                    04 398 9410

Simply decorated, like an upmarket art student's den without the tye dye, this is Dubai's only organic supermarket. This cafe on the side serves fine sandwiches, simple healthy salads, good burgers and the requiste herbal teas and juices. Prices are surprisingly cheap. Map 4 F1 48

# Restaurants

## Al Mallah                                            Arabic

Al Dhiyafah Street                                      04 398 4723

Al Mallah offers great pavement dining with an excellent view of the world and his brothers cruising by in their Ferraris. The shawarmas and fruit juices are excellent, the cheese and zatar manoushi exceedingly tasty, and it has possibly the biggest and best falafel in Dubai. The incongrous 'Diana' and 'Charles' shakes are recommended. Map 4 F1 49

## Coconut Grove                                        Indian

Rydges Plaza Hotel                                      04 398 2222

To the surprise of most first timers, but to not to old-hat converts, Coconut Grove is one of Dubai's best Indian restaurants. The chef prepares dishes using a mix of ingredients from Sri Lanka and India. The crab curry in tamarind sauce comes recommended, as does the saffron-flavoured rice. Alcohol is available. Map 4 F2 50

### Il Rustico
Rydges Plaza Hotel

Italian

04 398 2222

You don't expect to find quality, well-priced, Italian food by a roundabout in Satwa, but the food at Il Rustico is surprisingly good. A decent wine list accompanies some obvious staples but there are some good choices hiding among the lasagne and margarita pizza. The seafood specials are usually a good bet, while the thin-crust pizzas with rocket make a great starter to share. Map 4 F2 50

### Pars Iranian Kitchen
Near Rydges Plaza Hotel

Iranian

04 398 4000

Pars offers a traditional laid-back atmosphere a million miles from the modernity suggested by its neon sign. The menu is limited, but includes staples such as hummus, moutabel, tabbouleh, and a selection of grilled meats, kebabs and Iranian stews. Its delightful front garden, enclosed by a fairy light-entwined hedgerow, is home to low tables and soft, majlis bench seats, perfect for enjoying a leisurely shisha with a group of friends. Map 4 F2 51

### Ravi's
Near Satwa Roundabout

Pakistani

04 331 5353

This 24 hour diner offers a range of Pakistani curried favourites and rice dishes, alongside more quirky fare such as fried brains. The venue is basic, with most people opting to sit outside with all of Satwa life on show. Dining is also available in the main restaurant or in the quieter family section. A late-night takeaway favourite for many. Map 4 F2 52

### Sidra
Al Dhiyafah Street

Lebanese

04 345 3044

Sidra's neon sign never fails to entice foodies, especially those looking for the best grilled haloumi cheese this side of Lebanon. The menu might not set the world on fire but if you want good, reliable Arabic cuisine at prices that won't make you weep then pull up a chair at this pavement restaurant.
Map 4 F1 53

## Bars & Pubs

### Aussie Legends
Rydges Plaza Hotel

04 398 2222

Perhaps not the best choice for a sophisticated night on the town, but for sporting events (of course, cricket features heavily), free drinks for ladies on Thursdays and surprisingly tasty food, Aussie Legends will serve you well. There are pool tables and a weekly pub quiz, so if you fancy a taste of Down Under and reasonably priced beer then don the corked hat and head over. Map 4 F2 50

### Boston Bar
Jumeira Rotana

04 345 5888

This American-style pub is a bit of a pick 'n' mix and not a place for contemplative *Cheers*-style introspection. Loosely themed events throughout the week inevitably end up with dancing on the bar and drinks-deal induced rowdiness. There's decent chunky bar food to soak up the booze and super efficient service. Map 4 F1 54

# Sheikh Zayed Road

Downtown Burj Dubai is breathing new life into the city's most iconic strip. Come here for cocktails, elaborate menus and neon clubs.

## Venue Finder

# Cafe

## Cafe Bateel

Downtown Burj Dubai                          04 228 9770

Dates are big news in Dubai and here's a tasteful cafe
dedicated to them. There's a fine selection of Arabic coffee and
cakes, while dates find their way into most dishes: the pesto
pasta and couscous and date salad are recommended. There's
also a tempting collection of deli items for sale.  Map 4 D3 55

# Restaurants

### Al Nafoorah                                        Lebanese

Jumeirah Emirates Towers                     04 319 8088

The menu at this highly rated Lebanese is extensive, with
pages and pages of mezze and mains to tantalise. It's best to
come in a group and share the wide selection. After dinner,
you can take a stroll round The Boulevard, or sit out and enjoy
shisha in front of the looming Emirates Towers  Map 7 D3 56

### Asado                                             Steakhouse

The Palace Hotel                             04 428 7888

Striking the balance between impressive and showy, Asado is
a hotspot for meat lovers. Men will love the hefty steaks and
women won't fail to appreciate the ladies' menu (on which
no prices are marked) and luxurious ski lodge decor. From the
signature bife de chorizo steak to the feather-light chocolate
souffle, the menu is well planned and beautifully executed.
Map 4 D3 57

## Amwaj
Seafood

Shangri-La
04 405 2703

The minimal decor here cleverly depicts a marine theme yet remains refined. An immaculate sushi bar greets you, and the open kitchen allows you to watch tantalising dishes being prepared. The menu offers endless fish and seafood creations, and the vegetarian and meat choices are equally impressive, especially the foie gras. Adventurous diners should consider the tasting and set menus. Map 7 A2 58

## Exchange Grill
Steakhouse

Fairmont Dubai
04 311 8000

Peer around the glass partition at Exchange Grill and you're confronted by excess: outsized leather armchairs, art installations and a floor-to-ceiling chandelier. But the steaks here are some of the city's finest, pure and simple. The menu strikes a balance between classic and innovative. Both lunch and dinner menus offer the best quality beef, including an expensive but worth it wagyu. Each comes with clever condiments. The desert menu is killer. Map 7 E2 59

## Spectrum on One
International

Fairmont Dubai
04 311 8000

With probably the most diverse menu in Dubai, Spectrum on One caters for a variety of tastes throughout each course. It features both adventurous and familiar dishes from southern Asia, coastal Thailand, Japan, India and Europe. Taste them all in a few hours at the fabulous champagne brunch on Fridays. Map 7 E2 59

## Teatro
Towers Rotana Hotel

International
04 343 8000

For awesome views of Sheikh Zayed Road served up with fantastic food head to Teatro. The creative menus will please most diners, with standard Japanese fare alongside palate pleasers such as fresh pasta with lobster. Trendy design features and an impressive glass wine cellar complete the experience. Map 7 B2 60

## The Meat Company
Souk Al Bahar, Downtown Burj Dubai

Steakhouse
04 420 0737

This popular South African chain is much more than just a string of steakhouses. The well-planned decor matches the thoughtful menu. Start with a mezze platter of three appetisers then move on to a healthy lamb skewer with peppers, or an enormous steak with your choice of carbs. Even the burgers feel like fine dining. There is another restaurant at Souk Madinat Jumeirah (p.98), which has alfresco tables by the water. Map 4 D3 61

## The Noodle House
Jumeirah Emirates Towers

Far Eastern
04 319 8757

Tick your choice on the menu pad then wait for delicious dishes to appear. This busy restaurant is ideal for fuelling up before hitting the bars in Emirates Towers, or kicking back after spending at the boutiques. With a good selection of beers, decent food and attentive service, The Noodle House is a good bet for fast south-east asian food; the bakmi goring and spring rolls are recommended. No reservations. Map 7 D3 56

### The Rib Room

Jumeirah Emirates Towers

Steakhouse

04 319 8088

The deep red upholstery and dark woods create an elegant contemporary Asian feel at The Rib Room. The well-rounded menu has a host of hot and cold starters, numerous steaks and an array of seafood but, bizarrely, no ribs. Excellent service, a warm intimate atmosphere and delicious food make for a satisfying Sheikh Zayed Road experience. Map 7 D3 56

### Trader Vic's

Crowne Plaza

Polynesian

04 331 1111

This tropical chain is a great party spot. You can come for dinner (Asian-inspired dishes, plus some fantastic finger food) or just prop up the bar with one of the famously strong cocktails. Either way, it won't be long before you're dancing to the live Cuban band and vowing to take salsa lessons before the year's out. There's another branch in Madinat Jumeirah (p.98). Map 7 D2 62

## Bars & Pubs

### Blue Bar

Novotel World Trade Centre

04 332 0000

Jazz fans unite for some of the best live music in town. Hidden at the back of the Novotel, the Blue Bar has a relaxed, low-key vibe with enough 'it' factor to give it cred but without any delusions of grandeur. You can opt to either pull up a stool at the large square bar, or get cosy in one of the leather sofas and armchairs. Map 7 E3 63

Vu's Bar

## Cin Cin

Fairmont Dubai                    04 311 8000

Thick carpet, fat cigars and a hefty wine list await at this city centre spot. It may give the credit card a bashing, but if you are into wine then it is money well spent. The slick bar fills up fast with an upmarket post-work crowd. Light up, sit back and contemplate your fortune. Map 7 E2 **59**

## Double Decker

Al Murooj Rotana Hotel                    04 321 1111

On a Friday afternoon this could be your average pub in any town. Whether this is good or bad is up to you. With big screen sports, dangerously long happy hours and karaoke, many appreciate the relative charms this pub provides. Don't worry, you can wear your trainers. Map 7 A4 **64**

## Harry Ghatto's

Jumeirah Emirates Towers                    04 330 0000

The singing in this tiny karaoke bar starts at 22:00, so you've got plenty of time to muster up some Dutch courage, and then dominate the mic until 03:00. There are more than 1,000 songs from which to choose. You'll find a decent list of cocktails and other beverages, although there is only a limited range of bar snacks and light meals. Map 7 D3 56

## Lotus One

Dubai International Convention Centre        04 405 2704

If the great cocktail list doesn't impress you then the swinging chairs at this swanky bar might. The decor matches the menu: sleek and pretty expensive. This downtown bar, replete with glass tables and floors and fibre-optic lighting, is usually packed with suits out for a good time. With a live DJ and strong drinks, Lotus One is one for the weekend. Map 7 B3 65

## Nezesaussi

Al Manzil Hotel                             04 428 5888

This upmarket sports bar, home to the best ribs in town, has enough glam to keep women happy while the match is on. Tastefully decked out in memorabilia, without looking like a sporty Hard Rock Cafe, Nezesaussi might be a tongue-twister but once you've been, the name is hard to forget. Boasting South African sausages, lamb from New Zealand and Australian steaks, you might think vegetarians would struggle to find something hearty on the imaginative menu, but it's not all beer and beef. Map 4 D2 66

### Scarlett's

Jumeirah Emirates Towers                    04 319 8088

Scarlett's has a reputation as a pick-up joint, but if that
doesn't bother you (or actively appeals), then there's plenty
of fun to be had at this popular bar. With some gimmicky
themes on week nights (free drinks depending on the height
of your heels, for example), the bar is pretty good for a quick
lunch – the burgers are recommended – or late drink.
Map 7 D3 56

### Vu's Bar

Jumeirah Emirates Towers                    04 319 8088

The elevator ride to the 51st floor is an experience in itself
and when the lift opens you are invited into an intimate bar
that feels like a private members' club. The window space is
somewhat restricted but still gives you a fabulous view across
Dubai's sprawling metropolis. There's a strict dress code and
you'll need to make a reservation. Map 7 D3 59

## Nightclub

### Zinc

Crowne Plaza                    04 331 1111

If it's good enough for Carl Cox, it's probably good enough
for you. House fans flock to this slick hotspot, known for its
packed dancefloor and cabin crew clientele. With coloured
lightboxes, lots of seating and international DJs, any night
at Zinc feels like a party night. In the same hotel is clubbing
alternative, Tribe. Map 7 D2 62

# Umm Suqeim

**Beautiful bars with Burj Al Arab views and some of the city's best alfresco dining make this luxury enclave a must.**

More than any other area, Umm Suqeim defines expectations of Dubai. Its collection of the city's iconic attractions – Mall of the Emirates, Souk Madinat Jumeirah, Burj Al Arab and Jumeirah Beach Hotel – delivers endless dining and drinking, wrapped in a luxurious sheen.

There's more style than substance in places, but there are also some real gems. From the gastropub stylings of Left Bank (p.241) to the end-of-the-pier thrills of 360° (p.239), you'll find some of the city's best drinking spaces, while Pierchic (p.237) and Villa Beach (p.238) offer cuisine to match their stunning ocean vistas.

It would take months to visit every outlet in Madinat Jumeirah (p.165), but that's partly its charm: rock up, pick something you fancy and move on. Those who want to extend their night have a choice of showy clubs, including The Apartment (p.242).

## Venue Finder

Left Bank

# Cafes

### Almaz by Momo

Mall of the Emirates                                    04 409 8877

Mourad Mazouz, the man behind London's Momo and Sketch, intends to enagage every sense with this salon, juice bar and shisha cafe. The intricately designed space is open plan but has been divided into nooks and crannies, places where you can enjoy a mix of north African mezzes and tagines and wicked-looking but alcohol free cocktails. Map 3 B3 67

### Armani Caffe

Mall of the Emirates                                    04 341 0591

It's little surprise that the feted fashionista has a cafe in Dubai's signature mall. The space is beautifully designed, the contemporary Italian fare is served with flair and the clientele is fashionable – probably not the best place to head if you're hungover. Map 3 B3 67

# Restaurants

### Al Mahara                                          Seafood

Burj Al Arab                                            04 301 7600

Your visit to Al Mahara starts with a simulated submarine ride that takes you 'under the sea' to dine among the fish. 'Disembark' and you'll see the restaurant is curled around a huge aquarium. The menu is almost exclusively seafood. It's fine dining at its finest, with prices to match. Gentlemen are required to wear a jacket for dinner. Map 3 C1 68

## Chalet
Beach Road

International
04 348 6089

The interior of this Beach Road hangout is clean and modern, with no more than a dozen tables packed into the compact space. Beware the unisex toilet that embarrasses first-timers who think they've walked into the wrong bathroom. The menu takes diners on a world tour, with stops in China for noodles and India for curries, but most people are here for the sturdy Arabic offerings including shawarma and the usual mezze suspects. Chalet is a dependable choice for affordable Umm Suqeim fare. Map 3 C1 69

## Pierchic
Al Qasr Hotel

Seafood
04 366 8888

Pierchic has the best location of any Dubai restaurant. Perched at the end of a long wooden pier that juts into the Arabian Gulf, it affords front-row seats of an unobstructed Burj Al Arab, as well as Dubai Marina and Palm Jumeirah in the distance. The delicately presented seafood and famed wine list come at a price but what you're really paying for is the view, especially if you request a table on the terrace. Map 3 B1 70

## Sahn Eddar
Burj Al Arab

Afternoon Tea
04 301 7600

Those with normal-sized pockets won't get a better opportunity to inspect the Burj Al Arab. This is where you can slurp tea and nibble expensive scones at the base of the world's tallest atrium. There's an endless feast of delicious sandwiches, scones, cakes, sweets, chocolates and a pot of your choice of the finest fragrant teas. After, consider a drink at the Skyview Bar where there's stunning vistas 200m above the sea. Map 3 C1 68

### Segreto
Souk Madinat Jumeirah

Italian
04 366 6730

Segreto is tucked away, but once inside, its smooth lines, pristine presentation, and warm sandy tones give it a contemporary spin. Your dining journey can begin with sweet champagne cocktails (Dhs.95 a pop) and delicious breads. The food is aesthetically appealing, if a little lacking in consistency, while portions are more suited to a catwalk model than a prop forward. Map 3 C1 71

### Shoo Fee Ma Fee
Souk Madinat Jumeirah

Moroccan
04 366 6335

Some of the views from Madinat venues are breathtaking, but even as you walk out onto the terrace at Shoo Fee Ma Fee you'll still find the postcard-perfect view mesmerising. The menu is authentic Moroccan; this is the only place in Dubai where you can choose between roasted goat leg (for two), camel kofta or a mixed platter of grilled lamb, chicken and camel. Vegetarians might struggle. Map 3 C1 71

### Villa Beach
Jumeirah Beach Hotel

International
04 406 8999

The buggy ride to the restaurant's door reveals the killer attraction: you're a bun's throw from the ocean and the Burj

Al Arab. The beach-hut aesthetic has a Polynesian vibe but the food is mostly modern Mediterranean. The service is excellent, and although the scenery doesn't come cheap, the food is beautifully prepared and the wine list has been put together with care. Map 3 C1 **72**

### Zheng He's
Mina A'Salam

Chinese
04 366 6730

Zheng He's superb take on Chinese delicacies, together with its exquisite waterside spot, ensure a constant stream of patrons. Exciting combinations used in dim sum and mini-roll starters are divine and complemented well with tangy dips and sauces, while the marinated fish, stir-fried style meat and duck are all worth discovering. The wine list is as thick as it is pricey, but in terms of culinary experience you certainly get what you pay for. Map 3 C1 **73**

## Bars & Pubs

### 360°
Jumeirah Beach Hotel

04 406 8999

One visit to this Umm Suqeim hottie will leave you smacking your lips with joy – for this is what holidays were made for. Like a static carousel for grown-ups, 360° is a circular rooftop with a bar at its heart. The place boasts stunning panoramic views of the Arabian Gulf. Early arrivals (it opens at 16:00) can take their pick of low white couches and suck whichever colourful shisha they fancy. Sunset signals cocktails, beats and one of the city's best alfreso nights. Map 3 C1 **72**

## Après
International/Bar

Mall of the Emirates
04 3412575

To accompany its first indoor ski resort, Dubai has its very own alpine ski lodge in the shape of Après. Its divided into three distinct areas: a good-sized dining space, a comfortable bar area, and the lodge lounge complete with a cosy fireplace and a mesmierising view of the snow. Although it is hard to keep your eyes on your plate, the varied menu offers good wholesome fare including steaks and pasta – perfect for respite and replenishment after a hard day on the slopes. Map 3 B3 67

## Bahri Bar

Mina A'Salam
04 366 8888

Imagine you had the chance to design the perfect bar. For starters you'd include a stunning view, with windtower rooftops, rustling palm trees, meandering canals, the towering Burj Al Arab and sparkling ocean beyond. The bar could have rich furnishings, comfortable seating, and ornately engraved lanterns. On the menu you'd make sure a comprehensive cocktail selection was accompanied by wines, beers, and delicious nibbles. Map 3 C1 73

## Bar Zar

Souk Madinat Jumeirah
04 366 6348

This upper level of this slick two-floor bar is open in the middle so you can peer over at the band and drinkers below. The faux brick walls, art-house prints, the small terrace and laid-back sofas make for a relaxed urban feel. The drinks are equally eclectic: with beer cocktails (champagne or Smirnoff Ice with

Guinness) and traditional, yet potent, long drinks. Bar snacks include crab cakes and spring rolls. Map 3 C1 **71**

### Jambase

Souk Madinat Jumeirah

Cajun

04 366 6730

Situated just off the main entrance to the Madinat, Jambase's tempting selection of cocktails is enough to kick off a good night. There is an authentic 50s style jazz bar atmosphere created by the dark wooden interior and rustic lighting as a live band kicks out the jams. The vaguely art deco stylings plays host to completely contrasting evenings. Map 3 C1 **71**

### Koubba

Al Qasr Hotel

04 366 8888

One of the best views in Dubai awaits you from the terrace of this sumptuous cocktail bar, and, on a balmy winter's evening, you'd be hard pressed to find a better spot. The ever-changing light show of the Burj Al Arab, and the balconies and windtowers of Al Qasr hotel creates a magical setting.
Map 3 B1 **70**

### Left Bank

Souk Madinat Jumeirah

04 366 6730

While Left Bank's terrace allows romancing couples a peaceful retreat, the contemporary interior decor welcomes large groups with good tunes and a fine selection of drinks. The bar menu is made up of simple meat and fish dishes – the coriander burger is recommended – along with a selection of nibbles and plates to share. No reservations. Map 3 C1 **71**

### Uptown
Jumeirah Beach Hotel                              04 406 8999

Take the elevator to the 24th floor to find this small but perfectly formed bar. The cool interior is classy enough, but Uptown's USP is the outdoor terrace: it's a perfect spot for 'sunset behind the Burj' photo ops. Get there at 18:00 to take advantage of the half-price happy hour and cute little canapes. The menu features some mouthwatering mocktails and a selection of tasty bar snacks. Map 3 C1 **72**

### The Agency
Souk Madinat Jumeirah                             04 366 6335

With a veritable vineyard of the squashed grape on offer, even wine connoisseurs won't fail to find something quaffable here. Dark wood, exposed brickwork and perch-friendly seating complete the chic setting. Tasty tapas-style bites include spring rolls, spicy prawns and delicious olives. There's another branch in Emirates Towers (p.93). Map 3 C1 **71**

## Nightclub

### The Apartment
Jumeirah Beach Hotel                              04 406 8999

Look out, another champagne cork is popping and yet more photos are being taken for local society mags. Yes, you have arrived at The Apartment, home to a few high rollers and many beautiful people. This is the place for hip-hop and house, all served with lashings of bubbles. Map 3 C1 **72**

Clockwise from top left: Villa Beach, Bar Zar, 360°

Entertainment

Dubai can't compete with the cultural offerings of Europe or the US, but it's catching up, especially in cinema and live music.

## Cinema

Movie-going is popular in Dubai, although screenings are limited to the mainstream so you won't find too many arthouse offerings. The biggest cinemas include a 12 screen complex in Mall of the Emirates (p.162) and a 21 screen outlet in Ibn Battuta Shopping Mall (p.160) – the latter has the region's first IMAX screen. Mall of the Emirates also boasts the luxurious 'gold class' option for selected films with a smaller theatre, enormous leather armchairs and waiter service.

During the cooler months head to Movies Under The Stars (www.waficity.com) where each Sunday they show a free double bill of movies on a big outdoor screen from 20:00. Kick back on giant bean bags, order popcorn or pizza and enjoy the novelty of alfresco films in February.

Cinema timings can be found in daily newspapers such as *Gulf News* and *7Days* and listing magazines like *Time Out Dubai* (www.timeoutdubai.com). At weekends, there are extra shows at midnight or 01:00 – check press for details.

There are some common cinema annoyances: sometimes freezing air conditioning, people chatting to each other or talking on their mobile phones, Arabic subtitles and of course the heavy hand of the censor.

A definite cinematic highlight is Dubai International Film Festival (p.38). The event runs for a week in December across various locations and showcases an impressive mix of mainstream, world and local cinema, from shorts to full features. There's usually a good range of talks and seminars from actors and directors, including George Clooney who showed up in 2007.

## Comedy

Comedy nights in Dubai are popular with the expat crowd but events tend to be semi-regular, rather than weekly nights. The Laughter Factory organises monthly performances, with comedians from the UK's Comedy Store coming over to play various venues throughout Dubai, including Zinc (p.233) and Jimmy Dix (p.221). A lot of comedy is aimed at the expat crowd, so unless you're familiar with the comedian's country, you might not be laughing. Keep an eye on www.thelaughterfactory.com for details of future shows.

## Live Music

Dubai hosts a number of concerts each year, and as the city grows it attracts bigger names. Past acts include Missy Elliott, Elton John, Faithless, Justin Timberlake, Sting and Robbie Williams. The bigger names usually play at outdoor venues such as the Tennis Stadium, Dubai Autodrome and the amphitheatre at Media City. The amphitheatre recently hosted Desert Rhythm, Dubai's very own music festival celebrating cultural diversity in music with artists including Kanye West, Ziggy Marley, Joss Stone, Mika and Madness over two days.

In addition to acts at the height of their fame, Dubai also plays host to a string of groups that may be past their prime, but nonetheless provide good entertainment (think Human League, Tony Hadley, Go West and Deacon Blue).

There has been a recent rise in alternative and slightly lesser-known acts coming over for some sun including Groove Armada, 2ManyDjs and Soulwax. Another event that goes from strength to strength is the annual Dubai Desert Rock Festival (www.desertrockfestival.com), which Muse headlined in 2008. Keep an eye on 9714 (www.9714.com), a promotion, events and marketing company, and general arts collective for information on more upcoming gigs.

## Theatre

The theatre scene in Dubai has always been rather limited, with fans relying chiefly on touring companies and the occasional amateur dramatics performance. However, as the city grows so does its thirst for culture, and with an increase in modern facilities over the past couple of years, theatre lovers are finally finding something to cheer about. The Madinat Theatre (www.madinattheatre.com) at Madinat Jumeirah hosts a variety of performances, from serious stage plays to comedies and musical performances. Bigger events can be accommodated in the Madinat Jumeirah's arena – recent events include the production of Stomp and The Nutcracker Ballet performed by Ballet Russe, The Classical Ballet Company of Wales. Dubai's theatre space has been bolstered further with the opening of the Dubai Community Theatre and Arts Centre (www.dubaitheatre.org) in Mall of the Emirates.

Dubai Community Theatre and Arts Centre

# Profile

Rapid change and growing multiculturalism hasn't stopped the UAE and its citizens embracing a proud heritage.

Despite its obsession with shopping malls and mega projects, Dubai manages what some Arab cities fail to achieve: a healthy balance between western influences and eastern traditions. Its culture is still very much rooted in the Islamic customs that deeply penetrate the Arabian Peninsula and beyond. However, the city's drive to become a cosmopolitan metropolis is proof of an open-minded and liberal outlook.

Courtesy and hospitality are the most highly prized virtues and visitors are likely to experience the genuine warmth and friendliness of the local people – if you meet them, of course (less than 15% of the population is Emirati).

The rapid economic development over the last 30 years that was sparked by the reign of Sheikh Zayed bin Sultan Al Nahyan ('The father of the UAE') has changed life in the Emirates beyond recognition. However, the country's rulers are committed to safeguarding its heritage. They are keen to promote cultural and sporting events that are representative of the UAE's traditions, such as falconry, camel racing and traditional dhow sailing. Arabic culture as seen through poetry, dancing, songs and traditional art is encouraged, and weddings and celebrations are still colourful occasions of feasting and music.

Heritage Village

### Shisha

Smoking the traditional shisha (water pipe) is a popular and relaxing pastime enjoyed throughout the Middle East. Shisha pipes can be smoked with a variety of aromatic flavours, such as strawberry, grape or apple. The experience is unlike normal cigarette or cigar smoking since the tobacco and molasses are filtered through water.

Despite ongoing rumours that smoking shisha outside will be banned in the UAE it remains hugely popular. See p.182 for some of the best spots.

## Religion

The negative view of Islam that has affected many Muslims living abroad has not had a knock on effect in Dubai, where you'll find various nationalities, whether Muslim, Hindu or Christian, working and living side by side without conflict. To Muslims, like many other religions and cultures, the family unit is very important, and elders are respected for their wisdom. Many generations often live together in the same house. Islam is the official religion of the UAE and is widely practised. The Islamic holy

### Cross Culture

The Sheikh Mohammed Centre for Cultural Understanding (p.60) was established to help bridge the gap between cultures and give visitors and residents a clearer appreciation of the Emirati way of life. It organises tours of Jumeira Mosque (p.80), one of the few in the UAE open to non-Muslims.

day is Friday. The basis of Islam is the belief that there is only one God and that Prophet Muhammad is his messenger. There are five pillars of the faith which all Muslims must follow: the Profession of Faith, Prayer, Charity, Fasting and Pilgrimage. Every Muslim is expected, at least once in his or her lifetime, to make the pilgrimage (Hajj) to the holy city of Mecca (also spelt Makkah) in Saudi Arabia.

Additionally, a Muslim is required to pray (facing Mecca) five times a day. Most people pray at a mosque, although it's not unusual to see people kneeling by the side of the road if they are not near a place of worship. The call to prayer, transmitted through loudspeakers on the minarets of each mosque, ensures that everyone knows it's time to pray. In Dubai, the plan is to build enough mosques so that people don't have to walk more than 500 metres to reach one.

Islam shares a common ancestry with Christianity and Judaism, and many of the prophets before Muhammad can be found in all three Abrahamic writings.

While the predominant religion is Islam, Dubai is tolerant of many other denominations, and the ruling family has, on numerous occasions, donated plots of land for the building of churches.

During the holy month of Ramadan, Muslims abstain from all food, drinks, cigarettes and unclean thoughts (or activities) between dawn and dusk for 30 days. In the evening, the fast is broken with the Iftar feast.

All over the city, festive Ramadan tents are filled to the brim each evening with people of all nationalities and religions enjoying shisha, traditional Arabic mezze and sweets. The timing of Ramadan is not fixed in terms of the western calendar, but depends on the lunar Islamic calendar.

During Ramadan the sale of alcohol in most outlets is restricted to after dusk, while shops and parks usually open and close later. In addition, no live music or dancing is allowed. Ramadan ends with a three-day celebration and holiday called Eid Al Fitr, the feast of the breaking of the fast.

# National Dress

In general, the local population wear their traditional dress in public. For men this is the dishdash(a) or khandura: a white full length shirt dress, which is worn with a white or red checked headdress, known as a gutra. This is secured with a black cord (agal). Sheikhs and important businessmen may also wear a thin black or brown robe (known as a bisht or mishlah), over their dishdasha at important events. You'll sometimes see men wearing a brimless embroidered hat (kumah), which is more common in neighbouring Oman.

In public, women wear the black abaya – a long, loose black robe that covers their normal clothes – plus a headscarf called the sheyla. The abaya is often of sheer, flowing fabric and may be open at the front. Some women also wear a thin black veil hiding their face and/or gloves, and older women sometimes still wear a leather mask, known as a burkha, which covers the nose, brow and cheekbones. Underneath the abaya, women traditionally wear a long tunic over loose, flowing trousers (sirwall), which are often heavily embroidered and fitted at the wrists and ankles. However, modern women will often wear the latest fashions under their abayas.

Traditional dress on sale

# History

Dubai has packed plenty into the last
30 years, but its colourful past stretches
back a little further.

## Development Of Islam

Dubai's early existence is closely linked to the arrival and
development of Islam in the greater Middle East region. Islam
developed in modern-day Saudi Arabia at the beginning of
the seventh century AD with the revelations of the Quran
being received by the Prophet Muhammad. Military conquests
of the Middle East and North Africa enabled the Arab empire
to spread the teachings of Islam to the local Bedouin tribes.
Following the Arab Empire came the Turks, the Mongols and
the Ottomans, each leaving their mark on local culture.

## The Trucial States

After the fall of the Muslim empires, both the British and
Portuguese became interested in the area due to its
strategic position between India and Europe. It was also
an opportunity to control the activities of pirates based in
the region, earning it the title the 'Pirate Coast'. In 1820 the
British defeated the pirates and a general treaty was agreed
by the local rulers, denouncing piracy. The following years
witnessed a series of maritime truces, with Dubai and the
other emirates accepting British protection in 1892. In Europe,
the area became known as the Trucial Coast (or Trucial States),
a name it retained until the departure of the British in 1971.

Fishing nets

# Growing Trade

In the late 1800s Dubai's ruler, Sheikh Maktoum bin Hasher Al Maktoum, granted tax concessions to foreign traders, encouraging many to switch their operations from Iran and Sharjah to Dubai. By 1903, a British shipping line had been persuaded to use Dubai as its main port in the area, giving traders direct links with British India and other key ports. Dubai's importance as a trading hub was further enhanced by Sheikh Rashid bin Saeed Al Maktoum, father of the current ruler, who ordered the creek to be dredged to provide access for larger vessels. The city came to specialise in the import and re-export of goods, mainly gold to India, and trade became the foundation of the emirate's wealthy progression.

# Independence

In 1968 Britain announced its withdrawal from the region and oversaw the creation of a single state consisting of Bahrain, Qatar and the Trucial Coast. The ruling sheikhs, particularly of Abu Dhabi and Dubai, realised that by uniting forces they would have a stronger voice in the wider Middle East region. Negotiations collapsed when Bahrain and Qatar chose to become independent states. However, the Trucial Coast remained committed to forming an alliance, and in 1971 the federation of the United Arab Emirates was born.

# Formation Of The UAE

The new state comprised the emirates of Dubai, Abu Dhabi, Ajman, Fujairah, Sharjah, Umm Al Quwain and, in 1972, Ras Al Khaimah. Each emirate is named after its main town. Under the agreement, the individual emirates each retained a degree of autonomy, with Abu Dhabi and Dubai providing the most input into the federation. The leaders of the new federation elected the ruler of Abu Dhabi, HH Sheikh Zayed bin Sultan Al Nahyan, to be their president, a position he held until he passed away on 2 November 2004. His eldest son, HH Sheikh Khalifa bin Zayed Al Nahyan, was then elected to take over the presidency. Despite the unification of the seven emirates, boundary disputes have caused a few problems. At the end of Sheikh Zayed's first term in 1976, he threatened to resign if the other rulers didn't settle the demarcation of their borders. The threat proved an effective way of ensuring cooperation, although the degree of independence of the various emirates has never been fully determined.

## The Discovery Of Oil

The formation of the UAE came after the discovery of huge oil reserves in Abu Dhabi in 1958. The emirates has an incredible 10% of the world's known oil reserves. This discovery dramatically transformed the emirate. In 1966, Dubai, which was already a relatively wealthy trading centre, also discovered oil.

Dubai's ruler at the time, the late Sheikh Rashid bin Saeed Al Maktoum, ensured that the emirate's oil revenues were used to develop an economic and social infrastructure, which is the basis of today's modern society. His work was continued through the reign of his son, and successor, Sheikh Maktoum bin Rashid Al Maktoum and by the present ruler, Sheikh Mohammed bin Rashid Al Maktoum.

## Dubai Today

Not even market experts can keep up with the constant stream of new developments. Still, it'll be great when it's finished.

One of the city's most surprising aspects is its rather modest beginnings: the Dubai of today is nothing like the Dubai of 50 years ago. But where others take pride in their past, Dubai concentrates on the future. Construction is the only constant, with new billion-dollar developments announced almost every week. It 's little wonder that road maps are barely relevant from one year to the next.

## People & Economy

There is an estimated 150 nationalities living in Dubai. The population in 2006 grew each month by 24,000 people and that rate has been rising since. According to the national census, the population in 1968 was 58,971. By 2006, it had grown to more than 1.4 million. Expats make up more than 80% of the population, with nearly 75% of them from the Asian subcontinent. Much of this section of the city's population work towards building the massive skyscrapers that have come to define it.

Unlike Abu Dhabi, Dubai's economy has been weaning itself off oil dependence for the last few decades. Whereas 20 years ago oil revenues accounted for around half of Dubai's GDP, in 2006 the oil sector contributed just 5.5%. Today,

Clockwise from top left: Fairmont Dubai, Old Town, Jumeirah Beach Residence

trade, manufacturing, transport, construction and real estate, finance and tourism are the main contributors.

## Tourism

The development of high-end hotels and visitor attractions, in conjunction with an aggressive overseas marketing campaign, have made Dubai a popular holiday destination. Its hotels and hotel apartments accommodated 6.44 million guests in 2006, an increase of 5% on the previous year. The mix of visitors at present is roughly 40% business traveller and 60% leisure. Dubai is striving to reach its target of attracting 15 million visitors a year by 2010 and 40 million by 2015.

## New Developments

For every record-breaking mega development that is completed, three new ones are announced. Construction of reclamation projects, the Palm Jebel Ali, Palm Deira (www. thepalm.ae) and The World islands (www.theworld.ae), is underway. Nakheel, the firm behind these and Palm Jumeirah, recently announced The Universe, a series of man-made islands that will surround The World.

### Arabian Canal                          www.limitless.ae

A man-made 75km waterway that will run from the new Dubai Waterfront development, past Al Maktoum International Airport, before linking back up with the Arabian Gulf at Dubai Marina. It will be the largest and most complex civil engineering project undertaken in the Middle East, sparking a number of new waterside communities.

## Atlantis, The Palm    www.atlantisthepalm.com

The flagship resort at the end of Palm Jumeirah is opulent even by Dubai standards. Operated by Kerzner hotels, it will have more than 1,500 rooms, a water playground, stretches of beach, a dolphin conservation and education centre and man-made lagoon, all accessed by an underwater vehicle tunnel and monorail.

## Burj Dubai    www.burjdubai.com

Currently the tallest man-made structure in the world. Completion isn't due until early 2009. Estimations put the height of the tower at 700 to 800 metres, but the final figure has been kept secret. Surrounding Burj Dubai is Dubai Mall, which will be the largest mall in the world, probably until Mall of Arabia (see below).

## Business Bay    www.businessbay.ae

Business Bay is based around an extension to the creek that will stretch up to Sheikh Zayed Road at Interchange Two before continuing to the sea. It aims to become the commercial and business capital for the region. When it's finished, the development will be home to 220 towers.

## Dubai Metro    www.dubaimetro.info

This light-rail network will operate driverless trains on four lines, including two linking Al Maktoum International Airport and Dubai International Airport. The network will include trams on Beach Road and Al Sufouh Road. The RTA hopes that by 2020 the metro will handle 1.85 million passengers a day.

## Dubai Waterfront          www.dubaiwaterfront.ae

Dwarfing all previous developments, Dubai Waterfront will consist of more than 250 individual communities. Madinat Al Arab, another new 'downtown', will feature Al Burj, yet another of the world's tallest buildings. Phase one sold out (to selected developers) within five days for a cool Dhs.13 billion. The project is being developed by Nakheel, the firm responsible for the three Palms and The World.

## Dubai World Central          www.dubaiworldcentral.ae

This will be a self-contained urban centre, based around the new Al Maktoum International Airport. It will feature commercial and residential areas, a science and technology park and a golf resort. The airport is expected to handle 120 million passengers a year by 2050.

## Dubailand          www.dubailand.ae

This aims to be the world's biggest tourism, leisure and entertainment attraction. There will be theme parks, a Sports City, numerous hotels, a snowdome, Formula One World and probably the largest shopping mall in the world (Mall of Arabia). The Bawadi project alone will house 51 hotels.

## The World          www.theworld.ae

These 303 artificial islands in the Arabian Gulf broadly represent a map of the world. The islands, varying in size, have been offered for sale to individual buyers, who can develop them as they wish. The islands will feature mansions, villas and apartments.

Clockwise from left: Burj Dubai, Space & Science World, Sports City

Maps

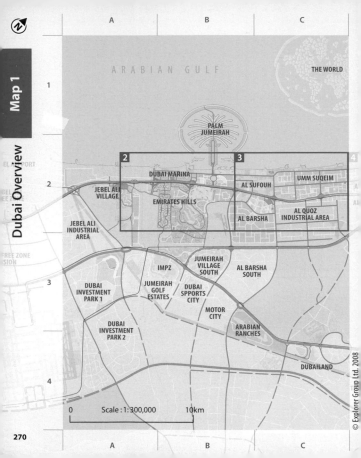

Map 1

Dubai Overview

ARABIAN GULF

THE WORLD

PALM JUMEIRAH

2

DUBAI MARINA

3

4

JEBEL ALI VILLAGE

EMIRATES HILLS

AL SUFOUH

UMM SUQEIM

AL BARSHA

AL QUOZ INDUSTRIAL AREA

JEBEL ALI INDUSTRIAL AREA

IMPZ

JUMEIRAH VILLAGE SOUTH

AL BARSHA SOUTH

DUBAI INVESTMENT PARK 1

JUMEIRAH GOLF ESTATES

DUBAI SPPORTS CITY

DUBAI INVESTMENT PARK 2

MOTOR CITY

ARABIAN RANCHES

DUBAILAND

0    Scale : 1 : 300,000    10km

© Explorer Group Ltd. 2008

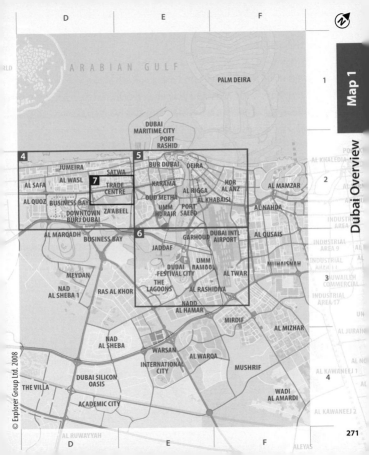

Map 1

Dubai Overview

ARABIAN GULF

PALM DEIRA

DUBAI
MARITIME CITY
PORT
RASHID

**4** JUMEIRA · SATWA · **7** TRADE CENTRE

AL SAFA · AL WASL

AL QUOZ · BUSINESS BAY · DOWNTOWN BURJ DUBAI · ZA'ABEEL

**5** BUR DUBAI · DEIRA

KARAMA · AL RIGGA · HOR AL ANZ

OUD METHA · UMM HURAIR · PORT SAEED · AL KHABAISI

AL MAMZAR

AL NAHDA

AL MARQADH · BUSINESS BAY

**6** GARHOUD · DUBAI INTL AIRPORT

AL QUSAIS

JADDAF · UMM RAMOOL

DUBAI FESTIVAL CITY · THE LAGOONS · AL RASHIDIYA · AL TWAR

MEYDAN · RAS AL KHOR

NAD AL SHEBA 1

NADD AL HAMAR

MIRDIF

AL MIZHAR

NAD AL SHEBA

WARSAN

AL WARQA

MUSHRIF

THE VILLA

DUBAI SILICON OASIS

INTERNATIONAL CITY

WADI AL AMARDI

ACADEMIC CITY

AL RUWAYYAH

AL KHALEDIA

INDUSTRIAL AREA 11

INDUSTRIAL AREA 9

INDUSTRIAL AREA 10

MUHAISNAH

UWAILEH COMMERCIAL

INDUSTRIAL AREA 17

AL JURAINA

AL KAWANEEJ 1

AL KAWANEEJ 2

ALEYAS

© Explorer Group Ltd. 2008

271

# Legend

These maps include what we feel are the most interesting bits of Dubai. Bars, shops, areas to explore and activities and spas are marked with colour-coded symbols (see below).

You may also have noticed the large pull-out map at the back of the book. This is intended to give you an overview of the city and highlights the main areas of interest, as well as sights and attractions. The perforated edges mean you can detach it from the main book. It'll come in handy if you and a travel companion have different plans for the day, or if you want to travel light.

**00 Essentials 00 Exploring 00 Going Out 00 Shopping 00 Sports & Spas**

## Legend

| | | | |
|---|---|---|---|
| H | Hotel/Resort | Land | Highway Road |
| 🏛 | Heritage/Museum | Beach | Major Road |
| ✚ | Hospital | Built up Area/Building | Secondary Road |
| | Park/Garden | Industrial Area | Other Road |
| | Agriculture | Water | Tecom ─○─ Dubai Metro (u/c)/ Metro Station |
| | Shopping | | E11 D92 Road Number |
| | Education | Cemetery | ⋮⋆⋮ Power Lines |
| ⛽ | Petrol Station | Exit 39 Highway Exit Number | ⋯⋯⋯ Emirates Border |

Maps

Street Index

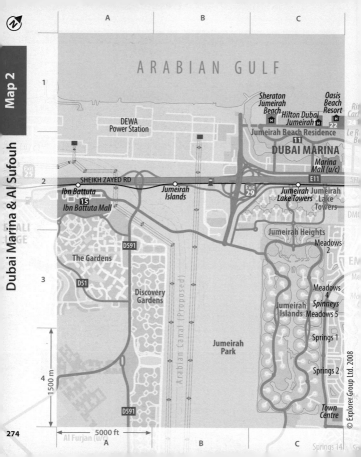

Map 2

Dubai Marina & Al Sufouh

ARABIAN GULF

DEWA
Power Station

Sheraton
Jumeirah
Beach

Hilton Dubai
Jumeirah

Oasis
Beach
Resort
22

Jumeirah Beach Residence 11

**DUBAI MARINA**

Marina
Mall (u/c)

E11

SHEIKH ZAYED RD

Ibn Battuta
Ibn Battuta Mall 15

Jumeirah
Islands

Exit
29

Jumeirah
Lake Towers

Jumeirah
Lake
Towers

DMC

Jumeirah Heights

Meadows
2

The Gardens

D591

D51

Discovery
Gardens

Meadows
4

Spinneys

Jumeirah
Islands

Meadows 5

Springs 1

Jumeirah
Park

Springs 2

1500 m

Town
Centre

D591

5000 ft

Al Furjan (u/c)

274

Springs [4]

© Explorer Group Ltd. 2008

ALI

EM

Me

Ri
Carl

Le R
Ba

Map 2

Al Fattan
Palm Resort (u/c)

Trump International
Hotel & Resort
(u/c)

The Trunk

**PALM
JUMEIRAH**

Oasis
Beach
Resort

Dubai
Promenade

Ritz-
Carlton

Habtoor Grand
Resort & Spa

Le Royal Meridien
Beach Resort
& Spa

Grosvenor
House

Dubai Intl
Marine Club

Tamani

The
Harbour

Le Meridien
Mina Seyahi

Westin Dubai
Mina Seyahi

AL SUFOUH RD

One&Only
Royal Mirage

ROOF UP
LOUNGE

Tulip Inn

DMC Boutique
Offices

Knowledge
Village

Holiday Inn
Express

Marina
Towers

Dubai
Media City

Radisson
SAS

Dubai Pearl (u/c)

SHEIKH ZAYED RD

Marina

Palm
Hard Rock
Cafe

Dubai
Internet City

AL SUFOUH 1

DMCC

Interchange No. 5

Nakheel

Emirates
Golf Club

Emaar
Business Park

Greens
Centre

The
Greens

Tecom
Millennium
Tower

Meadows 1

D61

**EMIRATES HILLS 2**

The
Views

TECOM

Sapphire

**EMIRATES HILLS 1**

Meadows 3

Ramee
Guestline

Montgomerie
Golf Club

The Lakes

Montgomerie
Golf Course

Jebel Ali
Racecourse

AL BARSI

Meadows 6

**EMIRATES HILLS 3**

Meadows 7

D611

1500 m

Springs 3

Meadows 8

Meadows 6

Springs 4

5000 ft

Springs 11

Springs 5

© Explorer Group Ltd. 2008

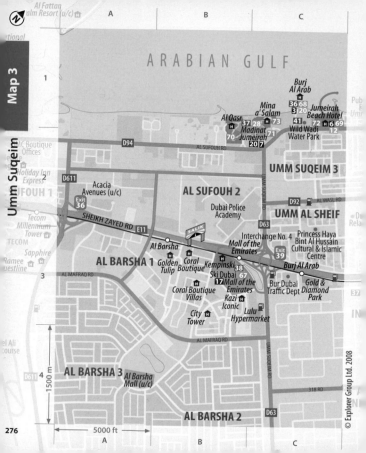

Map 3

ARABIAN GULF

Al Fattan
Palm Resort (u/c)

Burj
Al Arab
36 68
3 20
Jumeirah
Beach Hotel
72 6 69
12

Mina a' Salam
Al Qasr
37 28 73
70 Madinat
Jumeirah
20 7
41
Wild Wadi
Water Park
71

AL SUFOUH RD

D94

UMM SUQEIM 3

ABC Boutique
Offices

Umm Suqeim

Holiday Inn
Express

SUFOUH 1

D611

Exit
36

Acacia
Avenues (u/c)

AL SUFOUH 2

Dubai Police
Academy

D92

UMM AL SHEIF

D WASL RD

Tecom
Millennium
Tower

SHEIKH ZAYED RD    E11

D63

Interchange No. 4

Princess Haya
Bint Al Hussain
Cultural & Islamic
Centre

TECOM

Sapphire

Ramee
Guestline

AL MAFRAQ RD

Al Barsha

AL BARSHA 1

Golden
Tulip

Coral
Boutique

Kempinski
Ski Dubai
38 67
17
Mall of the
Emirates

Mall of the
Emirates

Exit
39

Burj Al Arab

Bur Dubai
Traffic Dept

Gold &
Diamond
Park

Coral Boutique
Villas

City
Tower

Kazi
Iconic
Lulu
Hypermarket

AL MAFRAQ RD

el Ali
course

D611

AL BARSHA 3

Al Barsha
Mall (u/c)

1500 m

AL BARSHA 2

D63

318 RD

© Explorer Group Ltd. 2008

5000 ft

A        B        C

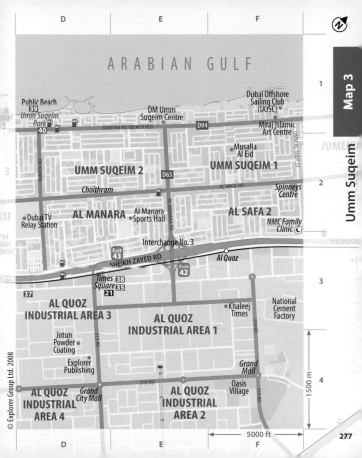

Map 3

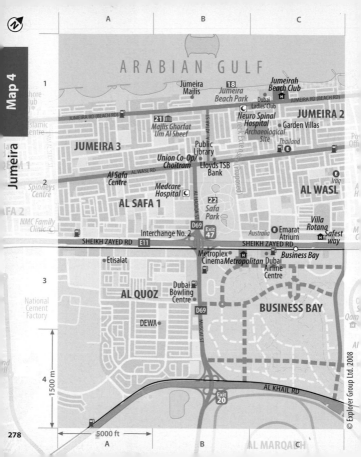

Map 4

Jumeira

ARABIAN GULF

A · B · C

**1**

Jumeira Majlis

**18** Jumeira Beach Park

Dubai Ladies' Club

Jumeirah Beach Club

JUMEIRA RD (BEACH RD)

JUMEIRA RD (BEACH RD)

Neuro Spinal Hospital

Garden Villas

JUMEIRA 2

**21** Majlis Ghorfat Um Al Sheef

Archaeological Site

Thailand

JUMEIRA 3

Public Library

**2**

Union Co-Op/ Choitram

Lloyds TSB Bank

AL WASL RD

AL HADIQA RD

Al Safa Centre

AL WASL RD

Medcare Hospital

AL SAFA 1

**22** Safa Park

AL WASL

Iraq

Villa Rotana

SHEIKH ZAYED RD

**E11**

Interchange No. 2

**D69**

Exit **47**

Australia

Emarat Atrium

Safestway

SHEIKH ZAYED RD

**3**

Etisalat

Metroplex Cinema

Metropolitan

Dubai Airline Centre

Business Bay

Dubai Bowling Centre

AL QUOZ

**D69**

BUSINESS BAY

DEWA

National Cement Factory

Qam

AL KHAIL RD

**4**

1500 m

Exit **20**

© Explorer Group Ltd. 2008

5000 ft

AL MARQAB

A · B · C

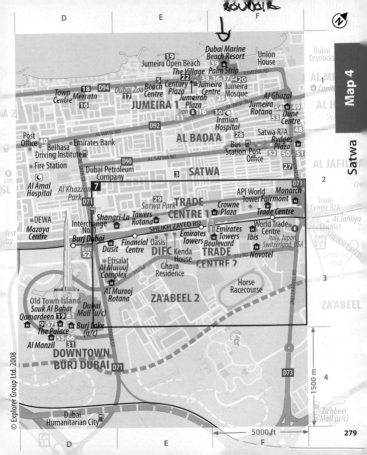

BOUDOIR

Map 4

Satwa

D  E  F

⊗N

Dubai
Drydocks

Dubai Marine
Beach Resort
Union
House
**19** Jumeira Open Beach  **39** Palm Strip
The Village  **22**
**5** Beach  Century  **38 36 37** **20**
**18** Dubai Zoo  Centre  Plaza  Jumeira Mosque
Town  **17**  Jumeirah  Centre  **11E** **16**  Jumeira
Centre  **16** Merrato  Plaza  Rotana
**JUMEIRA 1**  Iran  Al Ghazal  **54 49**
**30 C**  **53**  Dune
Iranian  Centre
Hospital  **48**
Satwa R/A  Rydges
**AL BADA'A**  **28**  Bus  Post  Plaza
Office  **40**  Station  Office  **52 50 51**
Post  Belhasa  Emirates Bank  **27**
Office  **40**  Driving Institute  **AL JAFILIYA**
Fire Station  **C**  Dubai Petroleum  **3**  **SATWA**
Company
Al Amal  Al Khazzan  **7**  **D73**
Hospital  Park  **29**  **TRADE**  API World  Monarch
**D71**  Satwa Park  **CENTRE 1**  Tower Fairmont
DEWA  Shangri-La Towers  Crowne  Trade Centre
Mazaya  Interchange  Rotana  Plaza  World Trade
Centre  No.1  **SHEIKH ZAYED RD**  Emirates  Centre  Italy, Japan,
Burj Dubai  Dusit  Financial  Oasis  Towers  Ibis  Switzerland, USA
Exit  Centre  **DIFC**  Boulevard  **TRADE**
**52**  Etisalat  Kenda  Novotel
Al Murooj  House  **CENTRE 2**
Complex  312 Rd  Ghaya
Al Murooj  Residence
Rotana  **ZA'ABEEL 2**  Horse
Old Town Island  Racecourse
Souk Al Bahar  Dubai  **ZA'ABEEL**
Qamardeen **19 61**  Mall (u/c)
**9 57**  Burj Lake
The Palace  (u/c)
**55 66**
Al Manzil  **31**
**DOWNTOWN**
**BURJ DUBAI**  **D71**

Dubai
Humanitarian City  **D73**
Exit
**18**

1500 m

5000 ft

© Explorer Group Ltd. 2008

**279**

Map 5

Bur Dubai, Oud Metha, Umm Hurair & Karama

© Explorer Group Ltd. 2008

PORT RASHID

Dubai Drydocks
Port Police HQ
Ports & Customs Authority
Highland
Carrefour
Heritage Village
Diving Village
Al Shindagha Tunnel
Al Ghubaiba
Ahmadiya School
Al Ras
Gold Souk

AL MINA
Capitol
AL HUDAIBA
Sea View
Norway
Abra
AL RAS
Souk Area

BUR DUBAI
Royal Ascot
Dubai Textile Souk
Bastakiya
Abra

Sri Lanka
AL RAFFA
Meena Plaza
Dhow Palace
Saeediya
Dubai Museum
Abra

AL JAFILIYA
Ramada
Netherlands
Four Points Sheraton
Golden Sands Area
Canada
United Kingdom
SAS Radisson Creek

China
Qatar
AL MANKHOOL
BurJuman
Saudi Arabia
Etisalat
Sheraton Dubai
Hilton Dubai Creek

Trade Centre R/A
Karama
Karama Centre
KARAMA
Pakistan
Jordan
India
Oman
Libya
Kuwait
Al Jafiliya
Etisalat
Za'abeel Park
Sudan, Lebanon, Yemen, Egypt

Karama Souk
UMM HURAIR RD

ZA'ABEEL 1

Malaysia
OUD METHA
Maktoum Bridge

Lamcy Plaza
Mövenpick
Al Nasr Leisureland
Oud Metha
Dubai Courts
Floating Bridge

American Hospital
Rashid Hospital
UMM HURAIR 2
PORT SAEED

Creekside Park
Dubai Creek Marina
Park Hyatt

Wafi City
Dubai Healthcare City
Park Hyatt
Dubai Creek Golf & Yacht Club
Aviation Club

Raffles Dubai
Healthcare City
Children's City

Al Wasl Hospital
Za'abeel Mall (u/c)
Al Wonderland
Grand Hyatt
Al Boom Tourist Village

Garhoud Bridge
Arabian

Map 6

Garhoud

N

Za'abeel Mall (u/c)

A

N Wasl Hospital

Grand Hyatt B

Wonderland 26

Al Boom Tourist Village

Golf & Yacht Club

We

C

Aviation Club 35

Arabian Park

Somerset Jadaf

Jaddaf 1

Culture Village (u/c)

Garhoud Bridge

Exit 59

Marsa Business Park (u/c)

14

Dubai Healthcare City Phase 2 (u/c)

1

Business Bay Bridge

Marsa Plaza

Marsa Auto Gallery

D83

Jaddaf 2

JADDAF

Crowne Plaza

InterContinental

30 5

Convention Centre

Dubai Creek

Festival Waterfront Centre 13 Ikea

Four Seasons (u/c)

Festival Power Hyper Centre Panda Ace

2

Dubai Opera House (u/c)

Marriott Vacation Club (u/c)

16

Al Badia Hillside Village

DUBAI FESTIVAL CITY

AL REBAT ST

RAS AL KHOR

Four Seasons Golf & County Club

8

Al Badia Residences

D83

3

THE LAGOONS

Al Badia Golf Resort

RAS AL KHOR RD

NADD AL HAMAR RD

NADD AL HAMAR

AS AL KHOR IND 2

4

1500 m

D62

Exit 23

5000 ft

A

Exit 25

Ras Al Khor Offices & Warehouses

B

C

© Explorer Group Ltd. 2008

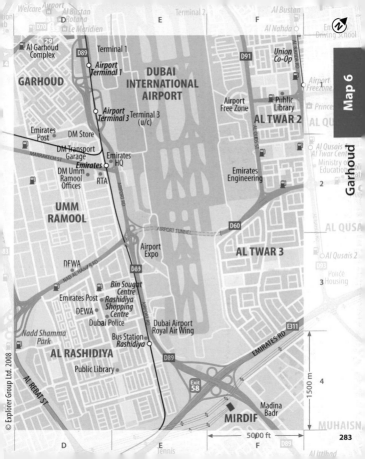

Map 6

Garhoud

Welcare Airport
Al Bustan
Rotana
Le Meridien

Terminal 2

Al Bustan
Al Nahda

Emirates
Driving School

Al Garhoud
Complex

D70
D89

Terminal 1

E

F

Airport
Terminal 1

DUBAI
INTERNATIONAL
AIRPORT

D91

Union
Co-Op

Airport
Freezone

GARHOUD

Airport
Terminal 3

Terminal 3
(u/c)

Airport
Free Zone

Public
Library

Prince

Emirates
Post

DM Store

AL TWAR 2

AL QU

MARRAKECH ST

DM Transport
Garage

Emirates
HQ

Al Qusais
Al Twar Cent
Ministry o
Education

Emirates

DM Umm
Ramool
Offices

RTA

Emirates
Engineering

2

UMM
RAMOOL

AIRPORT TUNNEL

D60

AL QUSA

DFWA

Airport
Expo

AL TWAR 3

Al Qusais 2

D93

D03

Police
Housing

3

Bin Sougat
Centre

Emirates Post

Rashidiya
Shopping
Centre

DEWA

Dubai Police

Dubai Airport
Royal Air Wing

E311

Nadd Shamma
Park

Bus Station
Rashidiya

EMIRATES RD

AL RASHIDIYA

Public Library

D89

Exit
58

1500 m

AL REBAT ST

Madina
Badr

MIRDIF

MUHAISN

© Explorer Group Ltd. 2008

D

E

Tennis

F

D89

500 ft

Al Ittihad

Map 7

Sheikh Zayed Road

N

D71

AL SATWA RD

1

14C

77A

6D

10D

81A

79A

77B

73A

71B

16D

22

77C

SATWA

10C

16C

57

57

51

6D

10B

53

49

20C

55

24A

28B

2

308 RD

30E

81B

79B

30L

69

61

Al Bada
Health Centre

Number One

Shangri-La

26 H 12

58

Karbasha

Exit
51

Wafa

Shk Ahmed

Kalantar

Al Salam

Towers
Rotana

Chelsea H

H 60

Financial
Centre

Doha

Satwa Park

Al Rostamani

Al Moosa 2

Al Moosa 1

Zabeel

Sahara

Al Safa

Emirates
Towers

SHEIKH ZAYED RD

Thuraya

Interchange No. 1

Al Kawakeb

Angsana (u/c)

21st Century

4

Oasis

Rose
Rotana

Gaya

Attar

Sky

Jumeira

Kenda
House

Capricorn

The Gate

Dusit

3

Burj Dubai
Business Hub

Dubai Islamic
Bank Towers

DUBAI INTERNATIONAL
FINANCIAL CENTRE (DIFC)

The Gate
Village

4

33

4

Etisalat

DOHA ST

6

Index
Tower (u/c)

312 RD

23

17

ZA'ABEEL 2

Burj Dubai
Square

Boulevard
Plaza

Al Murooj
Complex

D71

H 64

Al Murooj
Rotana

500 m

2000 ft

284

Dubai Mall

© Explorer Group Ltd. 2008

A

B

C

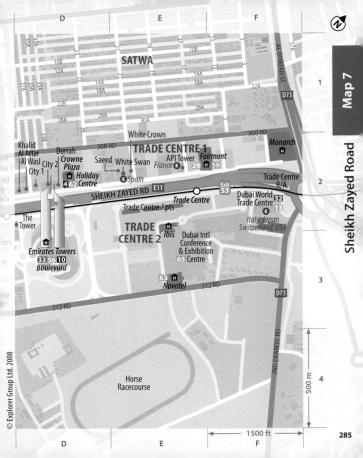

Map 7

Sheikh Zayed Road

D
E
F

1

SATWA

35A
35A
37A

10B
12A

14A
18A

22B
28A

14A
18A

28A

30A

10B

14A
18A

22A

300 RD

57A

AL DIYAFAH ST

D73

White Crown

Monarch

Khalid
Al Attar
Al Wasl
City 1
City 2

Durrah
Crowne
Plaza
Holiday
Centre

308 RD

TRADE CENTRE 1

Saeed
White Swan
*France*

*Spain*

API Tower

*Fairmont*
29 59

4 62

E

E

Trade Centre
R/A

2

E11

SHEIKH ZAYED RD

E11

Trade Centre

Exit
53

Dubai World
Trade Centre

32
13

The
Tower

Trade Centre Apts

TRADE
CENTRE 2

*Ibis*

Dubai Intl
Conference
& Exhibition
65 Centre

*Italy Japan
Switzerland, USA*

Emirates Towers
33 56 10
*Boulevard*

3

63
*Novotel*

312 RD

D73

312 RD

500 m

Horse
Racecourse

4

1500 ft

© Explorer Group Ltd. 2008

285

Index

# Explorer Products

## Residents' Guides

All you need to know about living, working and enjoying life in these exciting destinations

Coming in 2008/9: Bangkok, Brussels, Mexico City, Moscow, San Francisco, Saudi Arabia and Taipei

## Mini Guides

Perfect pocket-sized
visitors' guides

| | | | |
|---|---|---|---|
| Abu Dhabi | Amsterdam | Bahrain | Barcelona |
| Beijing | Berlin | Dubai | Dublin | Hong Kong | Kuala Lumpur |
| London | Los Angeles | New York | New Zealand | Oman | Paris |
| Qatar | Shanghai | Singapore | Sydney | Tokyo | Vancouver |

Coming in 2008/9: Bangkok, Brussels, Mexico City, Moscow, San Francisco and Taipei

## Activity Guides

Drive, trek, dive and swim... life will never be boring again

**Check out www.explorerpublishing.com/products**

## Mini Maps

Fit the city in your pocket

Coming in 2008/9: Ajman, Al Ain, Bangkok,
Brussels, Fujairah, Mexico City, Moscow,
Ras Al Khaimah, San Francisco, Taipei,
Umm Al Quwain

## Maps

Wherever you are, never get lost again

# Photography Books

Beautiful cities caught through the lens

# Lifestyle Products & Calendars

The perfect accessories for a buzzing lifestyle

**Check out www.explorerpublishing.com/products**

# Explorer Team

# Contact Us

## ▶ Reader Response

If you have any comments and suggestions, fill out
our online reader response form and you could win prizes.
Log on to **www.explorerpublishing.com**

## ▶ Newsletter

If you would like to receive the Explorer newsletter packed with
special offers, latest books updates and community news please
send an email to **Marketing@explorerpublishing.com**

## ▶ General Enquiries

We'd love to hear your thoughts and answer any questions
you have about this book or any other Explorer product.
Contact us at **Info@explorerpublishing.com**

## ▶ Careers

If you fancy yourself as an Explorer, send your CV (stating the
position you're interested in) to **Jobs@explorerpublishing.com**

## ▶ Designlab and Contract Publishing

For enquiries about Explorer's Contract Publishing arm and
design services contact **Designlab@explorerpublishing.com**

## ▶ Maps

For cartography enquries, including orders and comments,
contact **Maps@explorerpublishing.com**

## ▶ Corporate Sales

For bulk sales and customisation options, for this book or any
Explorer product, contact **Sales@explorerpublishing.com**

**EXPLORER**

DTC: 2080808
NATIONAL TAX: 3366611
CARS TAXI: 269 3344